AMERICA'S LIVELIEST GHOSTS
BY MICHAEL CONNELLY

– A Ghost Research Society Press Publication –

Original Cover Artwork Designed by
Jim Graczyk

This Book Is Published By
Ghost Research Society Press
P.O. Box 205
Oak Lawn, Illinois 60454
(708) 425-5163
http://www.ghostresearch.org/press.html

First Printing – August 2011
ISBN: 978-0-9797115-7-2
ISBN: 0-9797115-7-6

Printed in the United States of America

TABLE OF CONTENTS

INTRODUCTION

Everyone loves a good ghost story, but the reaction can be somewhat different when a ghost is actually encountered. The stories that follow are true. They are real encounters by real people with real spirits and the stories have been gathered by me and my late wife Kay throughout our travels as amateur ghost hunters. I use the term amateur because we did not carry any sophisticated sensor equipment or infrared cameras. A simple 35 mm camera and a small tape recorder were our tools, and our stories come from personal encounters with the unexplained as well as conversations with those who have had experiences or gathered tales of what has happened to other people.

Much to my delight, I have found that more and more people love to be scared and are fascinated by the idea of visiting haunted sites. As a result, I am often asked what it is like to be a ghost hunter and where one goes to find ghosts. The answers are simple. Ghost hunting involves only an open mind and a great deal of curiosity, and ghosts can be found virtually anywhere from old hotels and houses to battlegrounds.

In this introduction I will share many of the better locations for ghost hunting, some of which are dealt with in this book, and others that I have heard of over the years. If you love to travel, I hope you will take some time out along the way to seek out those who were in these places long before your visit, and who are still there despite being long departed from their bodies.

Many of our adventures have been in the west. The towns of Tombstone and Bisbee, Arizona abound with spirits as do places in the southern Arizona desert such as Tubac and the old mission at Tumacaroi, both just south of Tucson. Then there are the ghosts of Calico, California including the phantom of Dorsey the Wonder Dog.

Other western sites of note are the St. James Hotel in Cimarron, New Mexico, which has been featured on television's "Unsolved Mysteries" and other shows, as well as in my previous book, "**Riders in the Sky: The Ghosts and Legends of Philmont Scout Ranch**". The St. James has at least four active spirits. In Wyoming there are the ghosts who inhabit the Fort Laramie Historical site, and Kansas has the

"Blue Light Lady" who regularly appears at the Fort Hays State Historical site.

A visit to the Little Big Horn battlefield in Montana is well worth the trip since there are a number of lively ghosts there, as is the case with many battlefields. The most notable spot at the Little Bighorn is the area known as Reno's Crossing. The Chico Hot Springs Resort in Pray, Montana is also a notoriously haunted site. In Texas, the City of San Antonio boasts of many haunted locations including the Alamo itself and, you can spend days exploring the haunted sites in the beautiful border city of El Paso. Bandera, Texas and the surrounding Hill Country is another great place for ghost hunting.

In the Deep South you can visit almost any plantation home in Natchez, Mississippi and hear about their resident ghosts, and there have been extensive investigations into the haunting at King's Tavern, one of the oldest buildings in Natchez. North of Natchez on the Mississippi River you can tour the Civil War battlefield and plantation homes of Vicksburg where those who died in the siege of the city in 1863 are said to still roam. In the beautiful city of Savannah, Georgia there are ghosts in the pubs, the houses, and the cemeteries. It seems that almost everywhere you go you will find a haunted site and the residents of Savannah are very willing to share their ghost stories with you.

In the historic French Quarter in New Orleans, Louisiana there are ghost tours available almost every night that will take you to such locations as St. Louis Cemetery where the Voodoo Queen Marie Laveau is buried, and to pirate Jean Lafitte's blacksmith shop. North of Baton Rouge, Louisiana on State Highway 61 you can spend the night at Myrtles Plantation in St. Francisville, which claims to be the most haunted house in America. If you are in south Florida you may want to head for Key West and search for the ghost of Ernest Hemingway, along with the spirits of other prominent and long deceased residents.

Further north in Virginia you can take a ghost tour of Old Town in Alexandria, or cross the Potomac River into Washington D.C. where there are numerous ghosts including those who inhabit the White House and the U.S. Capital building. Also in the area are many Civil

War battlefields where the warriors of both the North and South are still said to be fighting for their respective causes.

These are just a few of the more famous locations. You can visit virtually any place in America and find haunted houses, historic sites, and urban legends. Don't be afraid to ask, because I have found that as much as people like to hear a good ghost story, those who have had experiences or know of stories enjoy telling them even more.

Good Luck and Good Hunting.

CHAPTER I

GHOSTS OF TOMBSTONE: THE O. K. CORRAL

It is a crisp October day in the town of Tombstone, Arizona as four men walk side by side down Allen Street, the small community's main thoroughfare. Their faces are set and grim, but their eyes are constantly moving, watching for an ambush as they approach the O.K. Corral. They know that death waits at their destination because the four men, Wyatt, Virgil, and Morgan Earp, and their friend "Doc" Holliday have been repeatedly threatened by the cowboys waiting at the corral. The Earps have had enough and what they hope will be the final showdown is about to occur. They are well armed for the confrontation because the Earp brothers have their side arms and Doc Holiday has a sawed off shotgun.

As the four men enter the dusty corral they are faced by five heavily armed cowboys, Ike and Billy Clanton, the McLaury brothers, Frank and Tom, and Billy Claiborne. There is no time wasted in idle talk, Wyatt and Billy Clanton draw their guns first, and the battle commences. It only lasts for thirty seconds and when it ends both of the McLaury brothers and Billy Clanton lie dead. Virgil and Morgan Earp are seriously wounded and Doc Holliday receives a slight wound to the hip. Ike Clanton and Billy Claiborne have escaped.

The most famous gunfight in American history has ended on October 26, 1881, but the war has just begun. On March 18, 1882 Morgan Earp is shot down while playing pool in what is now the Legends of the West saloon in Tombstone. His death sets off a rampage by Wyatt and Doc Holliday that results in twenty members of the Clanton gang being killed within eighteen months.

Now all of the participants in these historic events are long dead and buried, but Tombstone's dead seem to rarely rest in peace. Visitors to the O.K. Corral have often reported seeing a cowboy standing alone at the site of the gunfight. He appears for only a moment and then disappears. Employees have also reported seeing him sometimes walking slowly through the corral after if it is closed for the day. He leaves no footprints in the dust, and can never be found when the property is searched.

On my most recent visit to Tombstone I took a walk one night down the plank sidewalk on Allen St. It was late and the illumination of the street lamps only made the night eerier. I stopped for a moment on the corner where Morgan Earp is often seen. He also appears only briefly, and most of the time tourists will think the man dressed in black standing near the street lamp is one of the local residents wearing a period costume. However, they quickly change their minds when he steps off the sidewalk onto Allen St. and simply fades away in front of their eyes. I didn't see Morgan that night but I never felt like I was truly alone during my walk, despite the fact that the street appeared to be completely deserted.

Morgan doesn't always appear by himself on Allen St. however. According to local residents the place to be on a rainy night is sitting on one of the comfortable seats in front of Big Noise Kate's Saloon. It is between midnight and 2:00 a.m. that three cowboys will appear down the street at the corner of Allen and 5th St. where the Longhorn restaurant sits. They wear black slickers, the collars pulled up against the weather, and dark hats. One of them carries a shotgun. They always cross the street heading for the old Oriental Saloon, now a gift shop, but formerly one of the hot spots in Tombstone. It was a place where there was likely to be trouble on any given night. The three cowboys disappear when they reach the door of the Oriental.

No one who sees them has any doubt as to who they are. It is the Earp brothers on patrol, still watching over the streets of Tombstone as they did in 1881. It is not surprising that they stop at the Oriental first because according to Keith, one of the local residents, the Oriental can still be a lively place. He told me that one winter night as he walked past it he heard music and boisterous laughter coming from the closed and locked building. As he reached the door there was suddenly light and warmth coming forth, as if the door were wide open. He looked in and was surprised to see a saloon full of cowboys and saloon girls drinking, and dancing to piano music. He closed his eyes and shook his head to clear his mind of this illusion, but when he opened his eyes again it was still there. As he backed away the vision finally faded but

Keith knew that for a few moments at least, he had gone back in time and had seen Tombstone as the Earps knew it, over 125 years ago.

CHAPTER II

GHOSTS OF TOMBSTONE: THE BIRD CAGE THEATER

It sits on the corner of Allen and 6th Streets, an old forlorn looking building that was once the most boisterous entertainment stops in the west. It is the Bird Cage Theater, a gambling hall, theater, saloon, and bordello all rolled into one. For over nine years from 1880 until 1889, it never closed its doors. While famous performers such as Lily Langtree strutted on its stage, ladies of the evening took their customers to one of the fourteen velvet draped cages that hung from the ceiling, and high rollers participated in the longest running poker game in history. It lasted for over eight years.

It was not all that unusual for this simultaneous entertainment to be interrupted by a barroom brawl, or even more annoying, the sound of gunfire. One hundred forty bullet holes adorn the walls and ceiling of the saloon, a grim reminder of at least sixteen gunfights that occurred under its roof causing both men and women to make untimely trips from the Bird Cage to the cemetery known as Boot Hill.

When the Tombstone mines were flooded in 1889 the theater closed its doors and was locked up. For over fifty years nothing was disturbed and then it was finally reopened as a tourist attraction. It is a must visit site since it sits as it did over 100 years ago, its original furniture and fixtures intact, but augmented by such additions as "The Black Mariah" the original Boot Hill hearse, and hundreds of other Tombstone artifacts.

Stepping through the doors of the Bird Cage is akin to entering a time machine. You will immediately feel history close in around you, and many people feel that they are not alone, even if no one else is in the room. In fact, for some individuals the intensity of the presence of spirits in the Bird Cage causes them to immediately flee the building, never to return. This happened a few years ago to a new employee who while alone in the theater began to hear strange noises in the main dance hall.

As the young lady entered the room she could clearly feel the presence of other people around her, but could see no one. Yet the noise level increased and suddenly a fierce wind blew up inside the building, swirling her western skirt and almost knocking her to the floor. She knew abruptly that she was definitely not welcome in the old saloon. She fled into the street and started looking for another job.

On another occasion an employee was opening up early in the morning when she encountered an unexpected obstacle. She had no trouble opening the doors and entering the front of the building that contains an old bar and some of the "gilded cages" used by the hookers who worked the Bird Cage. However, when she tried to open the door to the main dance hall, it wouldn't budge. Since she knew the door had no lock, and had always been easy to open she tried several more times but finally gave up and called the owner. He came down to the theater but couldn't force the door open either.

He ended up entering the building through the basement and when he got to the dance hall found that a large roulette table had been pushed up against the door. The building had been securely locked up all night and there was no sign of a break in, yet someone or something had jammed the massive table against the door. There was one more enigma; the table was so heavy it took ten men to move it back into place.

Tables are not the only things that appear to move about by themselves in the Bird Cage. Bill Hunley, a long time owner of the old theater, has a gold coin collection that he is very proud of and which he keeps at his home, or at least he tries to. The set is often disappearing from his house only to show up in one of the drawers in the theater office. Apparently Bill is not the only one connected to the Bird Cage that values gold.

Even more mysterious is the poker chip that was part of a very valuable set, but was missing for years. Then one morning it showed up on the poker table on display in the basement bar where the famous marathon poker game had taken place. It was placed in a locked drawer only to disappear again and show up several days later back on the poker table. It was put back in the drawer only to have the same thing happen again. Finally, it was placed in a secure vault, but you guessed it, it made its way back to the table once more. This pattern has continued and one can only speculate that maybe Doc Holliday, or some other dedicated gambler, is sitting on a winning hand and needs that chip to raise his bet.

Cheryl Leavere was the manager of the Bird Cage when I visited it and she told me it was not unusual to open up in the morning to find the T-shirts in the gift shop tossed around, and someone is constantly rearranging the money in the old cash register. There is also an ashtray that is always kept on the bar in the front room. Every few days it will disappear and Cheryl said that no matter how hard she searches she can never find it. It's really no problem though because it inevitably returns to the bar a few hours later, perfectly clean. Cheryl pointed out that she never cleans the ashtray, but obviously someone still hanging around the saloon believes it is part of his or her job.

None of this seemed to bother Cheryl however; she is used to mysterious noises, moving furniture, and doors that open and close by themselves, even when they have been securely locked. She is well aware of the ghosts, and if necessary she even talks to them. One chilly Easter morning several years before my visit she and another employee were opening up when they decided they had time for a quick cup of coffee. They closed the front door, only to have it open again as they walked away. Nobody could be seen, but Cheryl said, "We're going to have coffee, close the door." It slowly closed but then stopped abruptly, leaving about a two inch gap. Cheryl raised her voice, "you heard me, we're going for coffee, now close the door." The door was then closed completely.

These are just a few of the antics of the ghosts no one sees. The Bird Cage really gets interesting when these same ghosts manifest themselves in various ways, often in front of those who are the least prepared for it. For example, a few years ago a camera crew was filming a documentary in Tombstone and had entered the Bird Cage in order to film in the basement where the poker room is located. The basement is also the site of the bordello room where some of the highest priced ladies conducted business. Prices in Tombstone for a liaison with one of the "soiled doves" ranged from as low as 50 cents in one of the hastily constructed cribs on Allen Street to as high as $40.00 in the Bird Cage. In fact, Big Nose Kate, the infamous girl friend of Doc Holliday, was one of these higher priced girls.

In order to keep the bordello room just the way it was when the Bird Cage closed in 1889 the door to the room is blocked by iron bars so that tourists can see into the room but can't enter it. However, an exception was going to be made for the camera crew and Cheryl was in the process of unlocking the barred door when suddenly the old cowboy song "Red River Valley" erupted throughout the theater. The music was so loud that it literally shook the building and was accompanied by someone signing in a stiletto voice that was ear piercing. The Bird Cage was searched for the source of the music, but no operating stereo system could be located and in any case, there was never a copy of that particular song in the theater.

It is entirely possible that the source of the music was Rose Callahan, the "Silver Rose" as she was called, who was a singer during the saloon's prime years. She can still be heard often in the Bird Cage, singing to the tourists, many of whom believe that it is just background music and are totally unaware that they are being serenaded by a ghost. However, Rose had never before reached the ear shattering crescendo that shut down filming on that particular day. Either she or one of her companions in the spirit world violently objected to the opening of the bordello room to non paying customers.

Speaking of the basement, one morning a perfect cigar ash was found on the floor next to the poker table. Next to it was a so-called gambler's match, lacquered to make it burn longer. These matches have not been made for years, but in the past were often used by such gamblers as Diamond Jim Brady, Bat Masterson, and Luke Short. Neither the ash nor the match had been present the night before when the room had been thoroughly vacuumed.

You never know who you might encounter when entering the Bird Cage. Some Tombstone residents claim that there are as many as twenty-six separate spirits haunting the place, and who can say they are wrong. Mysterious music is not the only thing that occurs near the bordello room. At the other end of the basement there is an old wine cellar with some of the original wine casks still in it. The small door to the cellar is also barred by an iron gate that is kept securely locked. Yet on several occasions video surveillance cameras have picked up the figure of a young woman in a dress from the 1880s who appears to leave the bordello room and walk to the wine cellar where, oblivious to the locked gate, she enters the small room. When the basement is investigated no one is found and the gate to the wine cellar is still locked. Perhaps the figure is Big Nose Kate, known for her love of the grape, who is seeking a nightcap.

If you are lucky enough to visit the Bird Cage don't be surprised if you see an old stage hand wearing a visor and carrying a clipboard walking from stage left to stage right. As far as he is concerned the Bird Cage has never closed and he is still responsible for seeing that the stage is set for the singers, dancers, and actors. Even if you don't see any of the ghosts that inhabit the old theater you may still detect their presence by the smell of cigar smoke, cheap perfume, or a sudden drop in temperature.

Some of the ghosts can be mischievous, some just mysterious, and others are downright sad. One evening an employee discovered a man still in the building at closing time. He was very upset, saying that he had lost his wife. The employee accompanied him on a search throughout the building, but there was no one else to be found. Then suddenly the man disappeared right in front of her eyes.

Then of course, there are the spirits who just seem to be looking for a drink. One of these is an old man in miner's clothing who is seen just around closing time. When asked to leave he politely does so, but not by either door. He just fades away, probably disappointed that the bar is not open and the gilded cages are quiet. Yet, he continues to come back just in case the Bird Cage reopens and decides to return to its glory days.

I didn't see any ghosts on my several visits to the Bird Cage, but I was certainly aware of the sudden chill I felt when I entered the dance hall, and the feeling of someone behind me in the basement. Of course, when I turned, there was no one there. However, I did have one physical encounter while in Tombstone. In the O.K Corral there is a separate building with some old photographs and one of the original cribs that the cheaper Tombstone harlots used to use to entertain guests along Allen Street.

When we entered the room my wife Kay, who was of both Irish and Cherokee ancestry and therefore more sensitive than most people to the spirit world, immediately told me that we were not alone, even though I could see no one else. I looked at some of the pictures and then as I crossed the room to take a closer look at the crib I felt a hand grab my posterior region. I turned to grin at my wife and realized she had already gone back outside. I just hope it was one of Tombstone's long departed hookers who made this advance and not one of the Earp brothers. That would ruin my whole image of the place.

Poker table in the basement of the Bird Cage Saloon in Tombstone, Arizona where the valuable poker chip continues to reappear

CHAPTER III

GHOSTS OF TOMBSTONE: BIG NOSE KATE'S SALOON

It is closing time in Big Nose Kate's Saloon, formerly the Grand Hotel, and one of the landmarks of Tombstone. The basement gift shop is closed, the waitresses have gone home and only the bartender is left to close up the rest of the building for the night. As part of his nightly ritual he pours himself a nightcap and sets it on the bar before starting his rounds that include making sure the whole place is shut down and then locked up.

This particular bartender has worked at the saloon for several years so he is not disturbed by the creaking of the old building, or even the footsteps he hears behind him. He also disregards the voices that seem to be everywhere, some of them whispering, some loud and boisterous, and he ignores them even when they call him by name. He is not bothered by the sounds of breaking glass coming from the main bar, or screams from the balcony since he knows he will find nothing when he returns to that area of the saloon.

It is clear that the ghosts don't faze this veteran worker, at least until he approaches the bar that night and let's loose a string of expletives that would make a mule skinner blush. He's put up with being pushed, tapped on the shoulder, talked to, and generally harassed, but this time one of the ghosts has gone too far. His drink glass sits empty on the bar, drained by the unseen hand of a thirsty spirit.

In Big Nose Kate's Saloon it is hardly possible to turn a corner without running into a ghost. They seem to occupy every nook and cranny, and they don't appear to be the least bit shy. No one knows how many there are, but for sure a lot of people have seen the Lady in Red, the faceless cowboy in the black hat, and the swamper. There have even been pictures taken that show misty forms hovering over the bar, or in the basement gift shop.

What is now the gift shop used to be the hotel bar at one time, but prior to that was the basement home of an elderly man who was the hotel caretaker. He was referred to as the swamper and after he spent long hours working in the hotel, he spent even more laborious hours tunneling from his dank basement quarters into a nearby silver mine shaft. According to local legends he took thousands of dollars in silver from the mine, and it may still be hidden in or near the basement somewhere. That could be why the spirit of the swamper frequently appears to both employees and guests alike. He is still protecting his investment.

At the time I visited Tombstone in 200 Steve had owned the saloon for a number of years. His first encounter with the swamper was when he and some other men were opening up the caretaker's old tunnel in the basement. They heard the unmistakable sound of someone wearing boots with spurs coming down the winding staircase behind them. They heard the footsteps reach the bottom of the stairs, but no one appeared. However, Tom, who is also known as "Chief," is a full blood Mescalero Apache who had recently gone to work in the saloon and on several occasions has seen the swamper coming up and down the stairs. Chief describes him as an old man with a long gray beard and stooped shoulders. It is probably his misty image that has also been seen by gift shop employees, and photographed in the corner by the tunnel.

On the other hand, no one knows if it is the swamper or another mysterious ghost that likes to get overly friendly with the waitresses in the saloon. They are a great group of young women who dress in period "saloon girl" costumes and bring back the days of old Tombstone. Unfortunately, they literally have to watch their "backsides" because one or more unseen spirits take great delight in patting the girls on the rear end while they are working. This happens in all parts of the old hotel and they have gotten used to the fact that they can never turn around and catch the rogue.

These antics may be those of the ghostly cowboy who has been seen by Linda, one of the waitresses, who heard her name called and turned to see a cowboy with a black hat pulled down obscuring his face. He was standing at the end of the bar, facing toward her and he faded away when she spoke to him. This same cowboy has been seen by a local real estate agent and others.

Then there is the Lady in Red, who was seen shortly before my visit by Lynn, another of the saloon waitresses. Lynn was sitting at one of the back tables, taking a break, when she saw a pretty brunette in a red dress emerge from the stairs leading to the gift shop. She did not recognize the woman who walked right by her and then abruptly disappeared. This lady may be the jealous type and therefore could be responsible for what happened to Linda on her first day at the saloon. She was sitting at the end of the bar when four empty cans sitting on a nearby banister flew off one at a time and hit her. She has also been pinched, pushed, and had a bow on the dress she was wearing repeatedly untied. If the Lady in Red was one of the Grand Hotel's original saloon girls she may be getting tired of all the pretty new competition that is around.

In most cases the ghosts in Big Nose Kate's tend to be friendly and even helpful. Take the case of the belligerent drunk in the saloon who was using profane language and insulting the ladies. Suddenly the area around him turned almost freezing and people nearby reported the hair on their arms and the back of their necks stood straight up as they felt a powerful, but unseen anger emanating toward the drunk. He obviously felt it too for he quickly left the saloon and never returned.

It is also not a good idea to tease the ghosts in the saloon. They may respond in ways you don't anticipate. For example, one evening before the basement was converted to a gift shop an employee named Judy accompanied another employee to lock it up. The old mine shaft was in the process of being opened up and the stairs were still the old set that was raised and lowered by a rope attached to a heavy concrete ball. When they entered the room Judy said "OK Billy Clanton, if you are here show yourself!" Immediately the lights were switched off and back on and the concrete ball began to swing ominously around the room. Neither Judy nor the other girl stayed long enough to see if Billy Clanton actually made a physical appearance.

CHAPTER IV

GHOSTS OF TOMBSTONE: THE NOT SO FRIENDLY GHOSTS

Most of the spirits who inhabit Tombstone and the surrounding area are friendly enough, if somewhat mischievous. You'll notice I said most of them. There are some spirits who can be downright mean, and others that are terrifying just because of their general demeanor. One such ghost is the Lady in White who inhabits the bridge on the Charleston Road that leads from Tombstone to Sierra Vista and the historic Fort Huachuca, Arizona.

The Hispanic lady is seen most often on rainy nights standing by the bridge looking out over the blackness. It is reported that during a flash flood she and her son were caught near the raging river when the boy fell in. She plunged into the surging torrent to try and save him and they both drowned. Only her body was ever recovered. She apparently continues to look for her boy and is repeatedly seen by travelers, many of whom routinely speed up when they approach the bridge in order to avoid a direct encounter with her.

Those few brave souls who do stop when they see her usually end up watching in horror when she immediately disappears before their eyes. This is not always the case however, because one man reportedly stopped and offered the forlorn lady a ride. She accepted with a nod of her head and climbed into the car. The gentleman tried to engage her in conversation but she didn't respond to his questions so he assumed she spoke no English. Then just before they approached the city limits of Tombstone the lady disappeared, leaving behind nothing but a very wet car seat.

Fort Huachuca is an interesting place in its own right. It was founded as a U.S. Cavalry post to keep the Apaches in check and was the home of the troops who finally brought in Geronimo, after chasing the wily warrior chief for years. It is now a modern army base and is also supposed to be the site of a large cache of Spanish gold, buried long ago in the Huachuca Mountains. The cave full of gold was discovered once, but then lost again, and the army no longer allows anyone to search for it.

On one occasion years ago when they did allow treasure hunters on the post for a short period, Steve, the owner of Big Nose Kate's was the post officer in charge of providing security for the searchers. One night he spotted a strange light on one of the mountains and sent three jeep loads of troops to investigate. They found nothing, but everyone suspected it was the spirit of the Spanish priest left to safeguard the gold. His presence has been known for years, and no one is exactly sure what he will do if anyone ever finds the gold again. Many people don't really want to find out.

In the building that was once the old Oriental Saloon in Tombstone there are now several shops, and also frequent outbreaks of ghostly behavior. These include a cowboy in a long black coat seen in the back of the old saloon, another man seen only as a reflection in a mirror, and someone walking on the balcony. One or more of these ghosts loves to rearrange the books offered for sale in one of the shops. At night they are on the shelves and the next morning they are neatly arranged on the floor. Sometimes it is only the books about Wyatt Earp, and at other times it is the books about "Doc" Holliday. On one occasion one of the spirits threw jewelry at a female visitor who was wrongfully, and loudly, claiming that the store manager had failed to return some jewelry to her that she had on consignment. There is so much activity at the Oriental that most employees are reluctant to stay by themselves after dark.

During my last visit to Tombstone Richard Wilson owned the Oriental as well as several stores in other locations including Madame Mustache where tourists can get old time photographs taken of themselves in period costumes. Someone obviously resents this since the costumes, neatly on their hangers at closing time, are frequently found thrown around the shop the next morning. One employee heard footsteps one night when no one else was in the store. She left and got a friend to help her search the place, but they didn't find anyone. After the friend left she heard the footsteps again and this time felt a presence so ominous that she fled the shop and quit her job there.

There have been several ghosts photographed in Tombstone, one in Big Nose Kate's Saloon that now graces a postcard, and another of two distinct ghostly figures in the Crystal Palace Saloon standing behind several people that were being photographed by a friend. I took numerous pictures while I was in town and one in particular stands out. In the Oriental I took three pictures of the balcony in rapid succession. Two of the pictures just show the balcony devoid of any people. The third however, shows the distinct figure of a person sitting in a corner. There was no one there when the picture was snapped.

Before leaving the fascinating town that's "Too tough to die", I must recount one other incident. On our last evening in town my wife and I were walking down Allen Street just at dusk, heading for the Longhorn restaurant when I saw a middle aged man in the uniform of a U. S. Cavalry Sergeant. He was carrying an old Springfield rifle and was crossing the street with a woman dressed in a long black dress as if she were in mourning. His hand was laid gently on her arm in what appeared to be an attempt to comfort her. I turned to Kay who was looking in a store window, and told her to check out these people in really authentic period costumes. When we both turned back the street and surrounding sidewalks contained no such figures. They were either ghosts or very fast citizens of Tombstone because they had disappeared within five seconds.

CHAPTER V

THE UNREGISTERED GUESTS AT THE COPPER QUEEN HOTEL

If you plan on going ghost hunting in Arizona as soon as you hit the border people will tell you that in addition to Tombstone you should visit the Copper Queen Hotel in Bisbee. It is located about 20 miles south of Tombstone on State Highway 80 and is nestled in the southern Arizona Mountains. As you drive through these mountains you will suddenly enter a small valley and be greeted by the sight of a beautiful little town built into the side of one of the mountains.

This is Bisbee, once a bustling copper mining town and now a well known tourist attraction. One of the buildings that stand out is the Copper Queen Hotel, built by the Copper Queen Mining Company and opened in 1902. It was designed as a commercial hotel for traveling gentlemen, and was patronized by such historic figures as General "Black Jack" Pershing and President Teddy Roosevelt. Now the hotel is a Mecca for tourists and hosts several "mystery story weekends" throughout the year.

It is also the home of at least three lively spirits, one of whom is apparently the ghost of a former "lady of the evening" who plied her trade years ago in the hotel corridors. She is still around long after her death, and is known to whisper erotic propositions to men who mistakenly believe they are alone in the hotel's elevator. She also, in her bawdier moments, will appear totally nude at the top of the staircase leading from the lobby to the first floor, laughing and waving a bottle of whiskey. This is, needless to say, rather startling to any guests or employees in the lobby.

These appearances are rare however because she normally spends her time on the third floor of the hotel, particularly in room 315. Imagine, if you will, that you are a traveling businessman asleep in room 315 at the end of a long day on the road. Then something awakens you and you open your eyes to see a beautiful young brunette wearing a sexy black dress standing over your bed. Slowly and sensuously she begins to undress for you as her gorgeous eyes lock onto yours. Then when you can stand it no more you reach for her only to have your hands pass right through her suddenly dissolving body. In a moment she is gone and you are totally awake. This experience has been reported by several male guests who I might add not only lost their desire, but quickly checked out of the Copper Queen in the middle of the night.

Bobbe Hossman was the Special Events Coordinator of the hotel when I was there and she was kind enough to take me on a tour. She had never seen the amorous lady herself but on one occasion when talking to someone on the third floor she was almost overwhelmed by the smell of the "Lillies of the Valley" perfume the young hooker is known to have worn. As Bobbe led me up the steps of the ancient staircase to the third floor I didn't encounter the perfume, but I did feel the temperature right at the top of the steps drop dramatically, even though it was mid July.

I took several pictures of room 315. When I developed them there was nothing unusual, however a picture I took outside in the hall shows what appears to be a woman's face peering through glass in the door leading to the outside staircase. There was no one at that doorway, at least not visibly when I took the picture.

Another long deceased resident of the hotel is an older gentleman in about his mid sixties, finely dressed, who was first seen in the early 1920s. He roams the hotel at will, and is often seen on the stairs or in the hotel lobby. Once he appeared at the front desk late at night scaring the manager on duty so badly that he left a note saying he was quitting, left the doors unlocked, and was never seen again.

There is a third ghost who is unique in that he is only seen by children. This is undoubtedly because he is a five year old boy who is said to have drowned years ago in a nearby river. His connection to the hotel is unknown, but his presence is repeatedly reported by young children staying at the Copper Queen with their parents.

One of the most prominent sightings was on Thanksgiving Day 1999 when a large family group was having dinner in the hotel dining room. As the dinner progressed the four year old daughter in the family kept crawling under the table, much to the chagrin of her parents and grandparents. Finally the mother and grandmother asked her what she was doing and the little girl explained she was playing with her new friend, a little boy under the table. No such youngster could be found, but the hotel staff had no doubt as to whom the boy was. They have heard too many stories about the elusive lad from children who had no reason to lie. The staff certainly wasn't prepared to discount that particular story.

The Copper Queen Hotel is a beautiful old Victorian building where you can receive elegant service in historic surroundings. It is also the only hotel I know of that maintains a "Ghost Register" where guests can record their experiences with the hotel's unregistered guests. The register is fascinating reading and contains page after page of stories that confirm the existence of the ghosts at the Copper Queen. Whether they tell of the smell of perfume, the sight of the elderly gentleman on the stair case, or the children's tales of a playful little boy, few guests seem to miss having some type of ghostly experience at the most famous hotel in Arizona.

CHAPTER VI

DESERT GHOSTS: THE TUBAC PRESIDIO

The history of the southern Arizona Desert is filled with stories of lost treasure, warfare, violent death, and of course ghosts. A prime example of haunted sites in the area is the Tubac Presidio about 30 miles south of Tucson. It was originally a Spanish outpost built in 1752 and over the years was destroyed by marauding Indians, rebuilt, abandoned, and reoccupied by Anglo settlers. It is now a thriving artist community where you can find Native American crafts in abundance, as well as many other forms of artistic expression. The old Presidio itself is a state historical site with the underground ruins of the old fortress, an old building that is now a museum, and a more recent school house.

The grounds of the Presidio are the home to a lot of spirit activity. The school house must once have been a lively place because visitors and residents report the sounds of children's voices and laughter coming from the vacant building at all times of the day and night, even when it is locked up. Volunteer workers at the Presidio have also reported seeing a man dressed in the uniform of an eighteenth century Spanish soldier, as well as several women wearing clothing from the same period wandering around in the museum. When they are approached they leave the building by simply walking through one of the walls.

These are relatively mild hauntings when compared to the little Spanish lady in the black dress and black shawl who has been terrorizing the area for years. I use the word terrorizing because she is not at all docile when it comes to her search for the lost Spanish treasure of Tubac. The Arizona Desert can be spooky enough at night, going from deathly silent to being punctuated by the plaintive cry of coyotes, or the sudden howling of a desert wind. It can become much worse if you are a resident of the area and wake up to see a little old lady purported to be no more than four feet tall peering into your window around midnight.

She can also be seen walking through the walls of buildings, standing by the railroad tracks and abruptly disappearing, or even apparently digging a hole under a mesquite tree. When approached the hole will be there but the lady will have faded away. No structure seems to be immune to her presence and ghostly footsteps are the norm during the night in many residences.

The treasure she is searching for consists of a silver chalice, a silver crucifix, and a pair of silver candlesticks that were originally the property of the Spanish Catholic Mission at Tumacacori. According to local legend the residents of the mission community abandoned it when their church bell was struck by lightning and knocked from the tower. Needless to say, the superstitious locals took that as a very bad omen.

The crucifix and other items were first buried by the priests at the foot of the altar in case the frightened residents returned, and the church was put into service again. Years later two Catholic Bishops and their servants came from Spain to retrieve the holy treasure, but before they finished uncovering the precious items they were said to have been stolen in the night by two elderly Indians who had been watching the excavation during the day.

The objects were never recovered, but long after the search was abandoned a Spanish Sergeant admitted to his wife Margarita that it was actually he and his brother, not the two Indians, who had stolen the sacred objects and buried them near Tubac. He refused to tell her exactly where they had been hidden however, and since his brother had later been killed by the Apaches he could shed no light on the location of the horde. After her husband's death Margarita searched in vain for the items because she believed that the souls of her departed husband and brother-in-law would be forever damned unless she located the chalice, crucifix, and candlesticks so they could be returned to Mother Church.

She searches still and the old timers around Tubac will tell you that if you hear a frustrated and mournful cry in the middle of the night, or find a mysterious hole on your property in the morning, you can be sure that Margarita has paid you a visit.

CHAPTER VII

DESERT GHOSTS: THE PRIESTS AT TUMACACORI

The incursions of the Spanish Conquistadors into the American southwest were resented by all of the Indian tribes, and the Yuma tribe was no exception. The Spanish first came searching for gold and silver, and they brought their priests with them to bring Christianity to the pagan Indians, whether the Indians wanted it or not. In all too many cases over zealous priests would try to beat Christianity into their native parishioners, and would "protect" them from pagan influences by virtual enslavement.

As more and more Spanish settlers moved in to claim traditional tribal lands for their own they brought Spanish troops with them to keep the tribe members in check. This was more than enough to infuriate the Yumans. They vented their wrath on the mission at Tumacacori with an all out attack despite the fact that by all accounts the priests at this particular site were a kindly bunch who treated their Indian parishioners fairly and with compassion. Everyone who lived and worked in and around the mission was killed with the exception of a young boy and girl who were taken captive. At first it appeared that the four Franciscan Priests had escaped the massacre, but they were soon located in a nearby patch of woods and slaughtered.

According to the two Spanish children, who later escaped their captors, the Indians camped late that night on the bank of the Colorado River. Around midnight they became very agitated, pointing across the river and whispering excitedly among themselves. It seems that on the other side of the Colorado there was a ghostly procession of the four murdered priests carrying lighted candles as if on their way to vespers. The Yumans quickly moved their camp, but thereafter any time any of the tribe members neared the abandoned mission they were greeted by the sight of the dead priests.

When the mission was later reoccupied one or more of the ghostly priests could be seen going about their business in the mission as if nothing had happened, and one of the priests was frequently seen conducting nightly masses in the empty church. All four are said to return faithfully during the festival of San Juan, their spirits carrying the candles that never seem to burn out, no matter how much time has passed. It is perhaps their continued presence that contributed to the final abandonment of the mission in 1848.

The mission is now a state historical site but lay forlorn and abandoned for many years. Yet, according to the locals the priests remained, and on more than one occasion cowboys seeking shelter from the cold desert night would place their gear in the sacristy, hoping for a good night's rest protected from the often harsh elements. Instead, they would awaken suddenly to find themselves bathed in a soft glow emanating from the Chancel and hearing a soft chanting coming from the same source. Then they would notice an old priest kneeling in the Chancel, accompanied by two acolytes. This would be enough for the cowboys who would quickly and quietly saddle up and look for another and less crowded place, to spend the night.

The old mission is located on the highway leading from Tucson to Nogales, Mexico and is beautifully preserved. I spoke with the rangers at the site and they said there was one live resident of the mission before the state took it over. An elderly prospector used it as his headquarters, having established himself in the vestry, where he resided for several years. When questioned, he would acknowledge that he shared the building with a number of ghosts, but pointed out that they were all "holy" and therefore were nothing to be afraid of. Of course, that was an opinion that might not be shared by everyone, particularly the Yumans.

The area residents also tell of another ghost connected to the mission. There is supposed to be the ghost of an old nun who died years ago at Tumacacori and who now acts as a guardian angel for those driving the lonely stretch of highway. She hitches rides from those she is seeking to protect, after all, who can pass up a nun on the side of the road. She then disappears from the car when whatever danger she perceived has been passed by the driver.

A much more legendary and sinister spirit is said to haunt the desert near the mission. She is known as La Lloroma, whose mournful cries have frightened residents for years. She is said to have been a beautiful young woman who drowned her unwanted baby in the river because she was jealous of the attention the child was receiving from her husband. Now she is condemned to wander the night, searching for the lost child. She is most often seen by running water and flooded mines, wailing in anguish for the baby she will never see again. Her screams are said to be so terrifying that grown men will faint at the sound of them.

What makes this legend so fascinating is that I have heard the same or very similar stories all over the southwest from San Antonio, Texas to locations in Arizona, New Mexico, and even Southern California. The stories may differ slightly, but the ghost in question is always called La Lloroma. This is unusual for a legend since they are often spread far and wide, but the names are usually changed, and the circumstances are updated to fit the time and place. This is not the case with this spirit and maybe someday I will be able to track down the original source of the story. I have reason to believe it actually originated somewhere in Mexico. One thing is certain; it is a story that is often used to successfully keep mischievous children from wandering off at night.

CHAPTER VIII

THE CALICO SPIRITS

Why is it that children seem so susceptible to seeing ghosts that adults can't see? I haven't found a definite answer to that question in my research, but I do know that children often see and even converse with spirits yet are seldom frightened by them. Take the case of Calico, California, one of the best preserved ghost towns in the United States. It was founded in 1881 when a large vein of silver ore was discovered in the area, and the site quickly became a typical western boomtown. It is now part of the San Bernadino Park system and during the day is a thriving tourist attraction just north of historic Route 66 near Barstow, California. It is also the home of a bustling community of the long dead including a ghost named Anne.

Anne is a little girl often seen at the well cared for Calico schoolhouse. She wears a white dress and peers through the schoolhouse window at the groups of children who are often taken on tours through the town. She is never seen by adults, but the children always report the little girl moving from window to window following them as they walk around the outside of the building. The description they give is always the same. The strangest part is that although the child never speaks many of the children instinctively know her name although neither her presence nor her name is ever mentioned by tour guides. No one knows who Anne is, or was, but she is apparently a delightful little spirit.

The town's General Store is another place where children have spotted one of the long time residents of Calico. On one occasion the manager of the store was assisting a customer who was browsing through the gifts and souvenirs. The shopper's young son began talking to someone in an empty corner of the room. The adults could see no one but when the little fellow was questioned he insisted there was a friendly old man there. He described him in great detail, even down to the mining clothes and gear he was wearing.

The most amicable of Calico's ghosts is Margaret Olivier, the last of the town's school teachers who is buried in the local "boot hill". Several years ago a couple from England was wandering the main street when they decided to visit the old school house. They were met inside by an elderly woman who greeted them warmly and conducted them on a tour of the building. She wore period costume, and was a fountain of information about the school and the history of the community.

After a lively conversation the couple asked if they could take her picture. She gracefully consented and the husband snapped shots of the tour guide and his wife standing side by side. A couple of weeks later one of the Calico staff members received an excited phone call from the couple who were back in England. They asked about the woman who had given them the tour and were informed that no such person worked in the park. They then explained that they had suspected this because when they had developed the photographs only the wife standing alone had appeared in the pictures.

One of the Calico attractions is the reenactment of a cowboy shootout in the downtown area. It was well done and my wife and I enjoyed the antics of the cowboys. After it was over we went into the general store to talk to several of the actors and find out if they had experienced any run-ins with the supernatural. One of them was named Bob Cloward and he had been living in Calico for three years at the time we talked to him. When he had moved to town he had acquired a house that was being vacated by a couple. The young wife was deathly afraid of the ghosts in the old place.

Bob was not concerned, he was just happy to have a place to live right in the town where he would be working. However, it didn't take long for Bob to learn that the couple had not been exaggerating about the house. The first night Bob spent in the house it was very windy outside and he kept hearing cans rattling in the basement. He assumed there was a draft so the next morning he entered the basement to clear out the cans and was quite surprised to find that there were none. In fact there was nothing in the basement or the rest of the house that could account for the noise.

Several nights later he began hearing footsteps come out of the living room and enter the bedroom. Yet when he turned on the light there was no one present and a search of the house found no sign of anyone. This went on until one night when he heard the ghostly steps continue through the bedroom to the edge of the bed. Before Bob could do anything he felt someone sit down on the bed next to him. He could see no one, but instead of going into a panic the cowboy said he simply told the ghost that he had to get up early the next morning and would the spirit please hold down the noise and the walking around. The ghost apparently understood because it left and never came in the room again. However, that didn't solve the problem of the apparition constantly turning on lights, the water, and even the stove in the middle of the night.

Bob and some of the other re-enactors have also seen a woman in a flowing gown walking the streets of Calico at night. She is often accompanied by the sound of piano music coming from somewhere nearby; however, there are no pianos anywhere in Calico.

Another long time ghost resident of Calico is Lucy whose house still sits on the main street. At one time it was open to the public and Lucy's bedroom at the front of the house contained her original furniture. One piece was a rocking chair that sat by the front window. An employee moved the chair to another location in the room, only to find it the next morning back in its original spot by the window. When the same employee saw the chair rocking by itself later in the day, it was decided to leave the chair where it was.

The house is now used for storage but Lucy is often seen through the front window by tourists as she rocks in her chair and watches the passing procession of humanity. She also objects to the doors being locked at night and employees usually find them unlocked in the morning. Lucy may also be the mysterious lady in the flowing dress walking the streets of Calico at night. She disappears when approached, but is apparently just looking over the town that was the family's domain for many years.

When my wife and I were in Calico we were escorted into the house by one of the staff members. Before she started to tell us stories of the elderly woman my wife Kay immediately felt her presence and commented that she sensed that Lucy was a very friendly spirit who was just reluctant to leave the home and town she loved.

CHAPTER IX

DEATH IN THE MINES OF CALICO

The silver mines around Calico, California were some of the richest found in the west, yielding over 75 million dollars worth of ore in the sixteen years of the town's existence as a silver mining location. Calico survived into the early 1990s because of borax mining in the area. There were numerous mines in and around the town with almost thirty miles of tunnels. For some, the Calico mines would yield fabulous riches and for others a lonely death. The latter was the fate of a young miner named McIntire.

Mac was a handsome young man in his early twenties who was good at his job as a dump car shover, and proud of the fact that he was making enough money to support his elderly mother who lived in Calico with him. One day there was a massive cave-in in the area of the mine where Mac was working. Tons of ore fell on and around him but he apparently didn't die instantly. His friends could hear him calling for help as they dug frantically to try and reach him, but they could never find him. Yet, they continued to hear him calling for days, even though there was no way he could have survived that long.

Officials of the mining company were so sure that his body would be found that they shipped in a white coffin for his remains, which sat in the General Store for years, waiting for a body that was never located. Over the next few years unnerved miners would often hear Mac's pitiful cries for help echoing through the mine, and sadly the young miner's mother would hear him calling for her at night. She would often be seen standing a lonely vigil by the mine's entrance as if expecting her son to appear at any moment.

In 1896 the last of the silver mines closed and only years later were reopened as tourist attractions. Both caretakers and tourists have reported hearing a young male voice crying for help as they wander the deserted shafts.

There are also constant reports of a presence being felt in another mine where a miner named Scotty died a tragic death. He had disappeared one day while working at one of the lower levels. Several hours later another miner was opening an ore chute to fill up his dump car. When only a few pieces of ore came out he peered up the chute with his light, only to see the body of Scotty, crushed to death in the ore. Now his ghost hangs out with the tourists, manifesting his presence so powerfully that some people immediately flee the mine.

There is a campground located right outside of Calico and campers often report seeing a mysterious light traveling through the mountains at night heading toward the outlying mines. Some speculate that it is Scotty or Mac still searching for a way out of the mountains, but after visiting Calico I have my own theory about the light. I think it is the spirit of Dorsey the Wonder Dog.

According to a story reported in 1914 in the "Keene Courier" a half starved Collie showed up in Calico one day and was found by Stacey, the town's postmaster. The postmaster took pity on the poor dog and fed and watered him. He expected the dog to wander off but it stayed and efforts to run him off were of no avail. The collie had the pitiful pooch routine down pat so Stacey gave up and grew to love the animal that he named Dorsey.

Stacey had no easy job since his route included delivering mail to East Calico and that required a tough seven mile hike through the mountains. Dorsey became his faithful companion on this journey, making sure to pick up any mail his master might drop along the way. The partnership continued for months until one day Stacey became very ill. There was no one else available or willing to deliver the mail so it was decided to send Dorsey with it.

A special harness was constructed and Stacey carefully explained to Dorsey what he wanted done. A note was sent in the mail pouch explaining this new arrangement to the miners. In record time Dorsey was back with the outgoing mail from East Calico and a note from the miners that the dog had made a successful run. After several more successes Dorsey was appointed the official mail carrier for Calico, and with a special U.S. Mail pouch made for him he delivered the mail on a daily basis.

He would allow no one to interfere with him, often circling several hundred yards off of the trail to bypass anyone he saw coming from the opposite direction. I believe the light seen in the mountains is just Dorsey the "Wonder Dog" making his appointed rounds and he can't be stopped even by death.

CHAPTER X

GHOSTS OF THE ALAMO

It was a hell of a fight. One hundred eighty five volunteers from Texas, and as far away as Tennessee, held off five thousand elite Mexican troops under the command of General Santa Anna for thirteen days before being overwhelmed and killed in an old Spanish mission called the Alamo. The battle became a rallying cry for Texans who later defeated the Mexican army at San Jacinto and won independence for Texas from Mexico.

The old mission is now a Texas shrine visited by thousands of tourists each year, some of whom have seen more than they expected. Ask virtually anyone who works in downtown San Antonio, Texas where the Alamo is located and they will tell you that it is haunted. The stories have persisted since shortly after the Alamo fell in 1836. Cowboys herding cattle near the decrepit old fort would hear ghostly bugle calls summoning the dead defenders to their posts, and sometimes while riding herd would hear the sounds of gunfire and the dreadful screams of the wounded and dying.

As the City of San Antonio expanded, the grounds of the Alamo shrank at the hands of real estate developers. Finally what remains was saved for posterity and turned into a protected historical site. Yet, the visitations have continued with many visitors reporting seeing a lone sentry standing watch late at night on the ramparts of the old chapel. Sometimes he is joined by the images of buckskin clad men at the entrance to the Alamo. They can be seen both standing guard and sometimes firing their weapons as if defending the bastions once more against the final assault of Santa Anna's troops.

The ghosts of Jim Bowie, the famous knife fighter, and Davy Crockett of Tennessee have both been seen inside the Alamo grounds where they died, as have the spirits of other soldiers of both armies. Kay and I could both feel more than just the presence of history as we roamed through the Alamo grounds a few years ago. We encountered several definite cold spots on the hot July day, and at one point Kay felt the briefest but unmistakable touch of an invisible hand on her shoulder.

According to an article in the San Antonio Express News published on October 29, 1989, guests at the nearby historic Menger Hotel can often see ghosts dancing on the walls of the Alamo. They are probably dancing to lively tunes played by Davy Crockett who was accomplished with his fiddle. Strange lights often appear at night in an old stone tower near modern day highway Loop 1604. The tower was once an important sentry out post for the beleaguered Alamo defenders. They are said to be the lights of the long dead sentries still manning their posts and standing watch.

The most haunting legend of the Alamo has been repeated for decades and is accepted as fact by many people who have heard it. Shortly after the defeat of Santa Anna at the Battle of San Jacinto a retreating Mexican general ordered his troops to completely destroy what remained of the Alamo as a final act of revenge. The deed was never accomplished however because as the sun set and the Mexican soldiers approached the mission with explosives to carry out their orders they were greeted by the spirits of the dead defenders who brandished flaming swords and reportedly shouted "Depart! Touch not these walls!" The enemy soldiers fled in panic and the Alamo still stands today as a shrine of freedom to Texans and people everywhere.

I have visited the Alamo several times and on my most recent visit I had the opportunity to talk to some of the people who work there and got some personal stories about their encounters with the Alamo spirits. I found it interesting that not all of the ghosts are of defenders of the Alamo. In the Long Barracks I spoke with Jesus (pronounced Hay-sue-s) who has worked in the Alamo for years and has had several encounters. One morning he said he was opening up the Long Barracks and was standing at the north end looking toward the south end where the theater is located, when he saw an apparition travel from one side of the building to the other. This is an often seen spirit that employees call the cowboy because of the long coat he wears.

On another morning before the Alamo was opened to tourists Jesus was at the south end of the theater when he saw the flowing dress of a lady behind a column. He went to search the area, and of course there was no one to be found. He told me that he thinks it is the ghost of one of the Daughters of the Republic of Texas. In fact, he believes that it is Clara Driscoll who is called the Savior of the Alamo. In 1903 when the Long Barracks was about to be sold to be used for a hotel, Clara used her own money to buy it. She and the other members of the group she founded also saved the Chapel and other areas and eventually got the State of Texas to take over the site and make it a permanent historical landmark. According to Jesus there is a portrait of this famous lady in the theater and she is wearing the same dress he saw that morning.

In another area of the historic structure he has heard a voice say "Sir" to him when there is no one there. He believes that it is the ghost of a young boy who haunts the area. He also told me of a rather frightening experience he had once involving his name tag. Since the spelling of his name confuses people it is often mispronounced by those who believe it is pronounced the same as the name of the Savior, Jesus Christ. He finally decided to just start calling himself Jesse and had a name tag made accordingly when he started working at the Alamo. One day he was standing alone in the Chapel area when his name tag was suddenly ripped off of him by an unseen force and then disappeared. He couldn't find it anywhere, and when asking other employees about it he was informed that the spirit of a Mexican soldier is often seen in that area. Jesus believes this long dead soldier resented his attempt to Americanize his name and was responsible for tearing it off. Now Jesus has a name tag with his real name on it.

Shortly after talking to Jesus I got similar stories from John Richardson who is also an employee of the Alamo. He related that many people, both employees and visitors, have seen the cowboy in the long black duster wandering throughout the grounds. He is said to appear not to like people very much and is decidedly anti-social. That must make things tough for this long deceased cowboy since the Alamo attracts thousands of visitors every week. John also told me that there have been numerous sightings of the little boy who is often seen looking out of one of the windows in the Chapel. No one has any idea who these two spirits are and what relationship they have to the Alamo, but they apparently have no intention of leaving.

I also interviewed one of the members of the Daughters of the Republic of Texas that works in the Citadel, the original chapel of the Alamo. She told me that people have often seen the figure of a

Franciscan priest wandering around in the Chapel. He is undoubtedly one of the original inhabitants of the historic site who was there when it was simply a mission and not yet the site of one of the great battles in American history.

The Alamo in San Antonio, Texas where there have been numerous encounters with ghosts over the years

CHAPTER XI

THE STREETS OF SAN ANTONIO

As haunted as the famous Alamo is, it is just the tip of the iceberg when it comes to haunted sites in San Antonio, Texas. According to the same article mentioned in the previous chapter; in the October 29, 1989 edition of the "San Antonio Express News" there are numerous ghosts roaming the streets of San Antonio, and some of them can be downright terrifying.

Ghosts are to be expected in a city as rich in history and multi-cultural heritage as San Antonio, however one does not expect to see a headless horseman except perhaps in a tale by Washington Irving. In San Antonio there is such an apparition, and he is seen frequently in the Botanical Gardens which was apparently the scene of his hanging.

Necktie parties in the old west had a tendency to be sloppy affairs that were often carried out by locals who had no firm grasp of the law of gravity. The theory was that a gallows was built to have the body fall abruptly from a specific height with the rope tied securely around the neck of the alleged bad man, and the weights on the gallows counter balanced so that the condemned's neck would snap cleanly and quickly. That was the theory, but the practice was often something entirely different. Particularly, since often a gallows was not even constructed. A rope tossed over a stout tree limb was considered just as effective.

Sometimes the victim of an impromptu hanging would just swing around, slowly strangling to death unless members of the audience took pity on him and either jumped on his body to add their weight to the rope or mercifully shot him. The latter was not done often since a bullet from a .45 caliber pistol fired at close range had a tendency to pass through a human body and lodge itself in another onlooker, which, depending on the identity of the newest victim, might necessitate an entirely new hanging of the unlucky shooter.

In the case of the headless horseman of San Antonio a bullet was not necessary. His hanging, the result of his acquisition of a horse belonging to someone else, was appropriately done with him on horseback. The noose was tied to the stout limb of a large tree and the horse was slapped out from under him. Fortunately for the cowboy the death was quick. He had his feet securely in the stirrups so when the horse bolted the body of the cowboy stayed with the animal but his head was snapped off and flung into the crowd.

The terrified horse, with the gruesome cargo still aboard, headed out of town for parts unknown but is said to often return with the rider in search of the head that disappeared without a trace. Their appearance can be a rather startling experience for those who visit the gardens with the intention of spending their day in a tranquil place of beauty.

Another headless figure appears in the Sequin area. This apparition is that of young boy who is not searching for his head but instead carries it around with him wrapped in a bloody blanket. He has caused quite a stir in a local chapel by appearing in the aisle during services, and is also said to visit the homes of local farmers. Speculation is that he was killed and beheaded during a Comanche raid in 1840.

In the southwest part of the city there is an event that is said to occur at exactly 11:45 every night that can shake up even the most skeptical. In 1932 there was a fire in three railway box cars parked on a railroad siding. The fire trapped a hobo, known only as Joe, in one of the cars. His dying screams filled the night and there were several attempts by railway workers to rescue him but the fire was too intense. His body was never recovered; however his screams are heard at the same time every night as his spirit repeats its futile efforts to escape the inferno that cremated him.

There was once an old abandoned house on Old Camino Real where a different type of tragedy occurred. An abusive husband killed his wife during an argument and then dragged her body to the basement where he buried her and attempted to destroy the body with the use of quick lime. He was caught but that fact has apparently produced no satisfaction for the ghost of his wife, whose weeping could be heard every night coming from the old building.

While guests at the nearby Menger Hotel report seeing ghostly sentries walking the parapets of the Alamo they are also often treated to the appearance of a variety of apparitions in the hotel itself. One of the most often seen ghosts is that of one of the hotel housekeepers who lived in a small house behind the hotel with her abusive husband. He eventually murdered her, yet she continues to be seen roaming the halls of her former place of employment dutifully trying to take care of the hotel guests and their rooms.

The most famous ghost in the hotel however is that of Teddy Roosevelt who right after the start of the Spanish American War used the hotel as his headquarters as he recruited tough Texas cowboys to join his famous Rough Riders. His ghost and that of some of his cavalrymen are reportedly still seen in the hotel bar where the men were plied with drinks to help entice them to join one of the most well known military forces in American history. While he stayed at the hotel the future President of the United States would signal his needs to the clerk at the front desk by ringing the bell from his room in Morse Code. This was his unique method of attracting attention, and the ringing of the bell continued long after he had died and even after the bell had been disconnected.

Another famous San Antonio Hotel is the Gunter. Room 636 is the most haunted location in the hotel. Many years ago a man staying in that room killed a woman, dismembered her, chopped the body parts up, and then tried to dispose of the remains by flushing them down the toilet. During this grisly process a hotel maid walked in on him and he fled the building. He was apparently not the brightest candle on the birthday cake however because the police quickly located him at another San Antonio Hotel where he had checked in under his real name. He was quickly tried, found guilty, and hanged for his crime. There have been repeated reports of spiritual activity in room 636 even after it was remodeled and converted into three separate rooms in an attempt to stop the haunting.

While in the San Antonio area I took one of the ghost tours and one of our first stops was at the San Fernando Cathedral where the ashes of the Texans who died defending the Alamo were ultimately interred. There is a shrine there and on the side of the church there are faces that appear in the outside plaster walls. When they first started to appear the walls were re-plastered but the faces reappeared. According to one old priest at the church this has been going on for over a hundred years. I stood at the wall and there are faces clearly visible.

The tour also took us to an area in downtown San Antonio where there is an old hanging tree near the old Court House where reportedly criminals were executed for many years. This is also the location of a massacre that occurred during one of the many battles that was fought over the years by various factions for control of the city. Many people are supposed to have died in this area and apparitions of men women and children who died here are often seen. The hanging tree itself draws most of the attention however because of the faces that appear in the bark of the tree limbs. I saw several of these faces and got a very good picture of one of them. There is also another hanging tree in front of the old City Hall where it is reported that 300 Spanish soldiers were hanged in one day in the course of a few hours. The ghosts of some of these soldiers are seen both inside and outside of the building.

The next stop on the tour was a beautiful old building called the Spanish Governor's Palace that was constructed sometime in the early 1700s. No one knows why it is called the Governor's Palace since no Spanish Governor ever lived there, but it did house the Captain of the Spanish Presidio. This officer was in charge of the garrison guarding the Mission San Antonio de Valero which is now better known as the Alamo. At one point a little girl, apparently the daughter of the Captain or another officer, is said to have disappeared there. She was not found until several years later when a maid working in the Palace was killed by raiding bandits. The maid's body was dumped in a well just outside of the building and when her body was recovered the body of the little girl was also found in the well.

It is not known if the child was murdered or just accidently fell in the well and drowned. In any case, her body was eventually interred in the wall of the Governor's Palace and there was also a small alter constructed in the area where the maid was killed. The little girl's spirit is frequently seen playing in the courtyard near the well. The ghost of a young Spanish woman is also seen sitting near the well weeping and this is believed to be spirit of the young maid. In addition, there have been reports of the sounds of a woman weeping both in and outside of the building.

One of the most fascinating stories told about the San Antonio area involves one of the first Spanish Catholic Priests who came to the area to bring Christianity to the local Indian tribes. He met with the members of one of the tribes and began to tell them stories about Jesus

Christ. However, he was interrupted by members of the tribe who said that they had already heard these stories from a mysterious "Lady in Blue" who had previously visited the tribe on several occasions and told them all about Christianity. The priest was obviously confused by this because as far as he knew he was the first missionary to visit the area. He didn't learn any more about the lady until he returned to Spain and heard about a nun in a convent who was reported to often go to sleep for several days at a time. When she would emerge from this comatose state she would tell her fellow nuns that while she slept she was actually in the New World teaching Indians about the Christian religion. This had apparently been going on for a period of almost 20 years.

A portrait had been painted of the nun and when the priest returned to Texas he brought the portrait with him and showed it to the chief of the tribe. The chief positively identified the lady in the portrait as the woman who had visited them and instructed them in the ways of the church.

The outside wall of the San Fernando Cathedral in San Antonio where faces
of those killed at the Alamo appear

CHAPTER XII

THE ANCIENT ONES

They are known as the "Ancient Ones," a tribe of Indians who have puzzled archeologists for years. They were the Anasazi, and no one is quite sure where they came from or when they arrived in what is now the southwestern United States. They were an advanced civilization for their time, living peacefully for centuries in well constructed villages throughout modern day New Mexico, Arizona, and Colorado.

Then sometime in the twelfth century something went terribly wrong. The Anasazi became a frightened people, abandoning their traditional homes for fortified cliff dwellings like those found at Mesa Verde in Colorado. There they lived in apparent abject fear for decades until they abruptly disappeared. There is no clear evidence as to what happened to these proud people although recent archeological finds have uncovered evidence of cannibalism and torture.

Did some form of madness overtake this peaceful tribe causing them to turn on each other, or was it an invasion of some warlike tribe like the Toltec from Mexico that led to the demise of the Anasazi? Both of these are possibilities, although unproven, yet, there is another possibility that is whispered about among westerners and that enters the realm of the supernatural. It centers on a place in New Mexico known as Urraca Mesa that is now part of the 137,000 acre Philmont Scout Ranch, owned and operated by the Boy Scouts of America. Thousands of scouts come every year to backpack in the beautiful mountains where history is alive. This is an area known for its hauntings and other supernatural activity. The mesa is taboo to the local tribes such as the Utes and Jicarilla Apaches since some of the tribe members believe the mesa is the gateway to hell.

The legend arose over 200 years ago when the Navajo Indians moved into the area and briefly occupied the mesa. They did not stay long because they found ancient Anasazi petroglyphs that led them to believe that there had once been a great battle on the site. According to legend, the battle had been fought between the Lord of the Outerworld and his evil brother, the Lord of the Underworld. The prize they struggled so fiercely for was no less than the souls of the Ancient Ones, the Anasazi themselves. The battle was vicious and ended with the Lord of the Outerworld being victorious and banishing his sibling and his evil minions back to the nether regions, at least for the time being.

To guard against his return and the escape of the demons he controlled, the Navajo surrounded the mesa with sacred carved cat totems and left their most powerful Shaman to protect the totems from destruction so the gateway would be kept closed. According to the local tribes and many visitors to the mesa, the Shaman still stands guard today. His spirit is often seen bathed in a blue light and sometimes appearing in his full Shaman regalia, or as one of his alter egos such as a panther or a bear.

Yet, there is speculation that his vigil started too late to save the Anasazi people. Could it be that the demons made good their escape once again long enough to hunt down and claim the Ancient Ones for the underworld after all? It is another possible explanation for the unexplainable and makes one hope that the Navajo Shaman will continue to maintain his lonely watch. If the demons escape again who knows what souls they will seek out this time.

CHAPTER XIII

THE WARRIOR SPIRITS

Anyone who has studied the history of American Indian tribes will tell you of the amazing spirituality of these native people. They were in touch not only with their own spirits but the spirits of the things around them such as the earth, the animals, and even the elements. Their descendents still are, and my own experiences have shown me that the spirits of many of the departed warriors are still around.

The Boy Scouts of America have always had a special regard for the history and culture of the American Indian. The Boy Scout honor society is called the Order of the Arrow and initiates are required to go through a period of testing and a sacred ceremony taught to the scouts many years ago by one of the tribes. The society is organized into lodges and many of these Lodges of the Order of the Arrow have Indian dance teams made up of members who make their own authentic regalia and perform dances taken from the various tribes. The troop I was scoutmaster of in Baton Rouge was Troop 888, and it had enough OA members to have its own dance team that performed all over Louisiana and often competed in Pow Wows against teams from local tribes.

The boys always had a reverent attitude toward what they were doing because they were well aware that they were dealing with a culture that is an intricate and very special part of our country's heritage. We first began to realize how special it is one chilly night in January 1994 when our team was invited to perform at a Mardi Gras ball just outside of Baton Rouge. I was frankly a little concerned about the prospect since Mardi Gras balls are generally not sober affairs, but tend to be very boisterous. However, it was a rare chance for the boys to show their dancing skills in front of several thousand people at one time so we decided to do it.

On the night of the ball we arrived at the location early, set up the drums and had the boys put on their regalia. The first dance was the Winnebago War Dance which is a complicated dance with six dancers and the drummers performing. The dance was well received and the crowd was very respectful. Then there were introductions of the Mardi

Gras Royalty and some other entertainment before my son Sean was called upon to do the Eagle Dance. This is one of the most important dances among American Indians with many different tribes having some version of it. Sean was very good at it, but by now the crowd had become more boisterous than ever with the alcohol continuing to flow freely.

As the dance was announced it appeared as if many people had not even heard the announcement and the noise hardly abated as Sean walked into the middle of the huge ballroom floor. The drummers started their cadence and Sean began doing the intricate moves that he spent many hours practicing. Suddenly the entire auditorium became quiet as all eyes turned to the lone dancer in the middle of the huge room. The audience was captivated, silent, and reverent. Sean seemed unaware of the change as his movements became more rapid and more fluid. He danced like he had never danced before and when he finished and the drums stopped nothing happened for a few seconds. Then, as if several thousand people had awakened at one time from a trance, the audience erupted into a standing ovation. Sean acknowledged the adoration of the crowd for a moment and then walked off of the floor. As he passed me he said nothing but our eyes met and we both knew that something extraordinary had happened that night. He had not been alone on that dance floor.

That was the first time we had an experience like that, but it would not be the last. Our scout troop was very proud of the fact that we had a large number of Eagle Scouts and all of them were also members of the Order of the Arrow. As scouts earned the rank of Eagle they became eligible to join a very special group within the troop, the Eagle Clan. We would hold a ceremony every few months to initiate new Eagles into the clan and several of these ceremonies provided some experiences that the clan members would not forget.

On one occasion we held the ceremony during a campout at the Avondale Scout Camp that was a few miles north of Baton Rouge. At around 11 p.m. we took the new Eagles to be initiated deep into the woods where we built a campfire. Then we sat around the fire and used the ceremony we had developed ourselves to bring the new boys into the clan. It was a very still night and there was not even a puff of breeze. As a result the smoke from the small campfire was curling straight up into the air. Part of the ceremony was always to pass around the peace pipe that had been made during one of our Boy Scout summer camps from a piece of the sacred black stone that came from the Black Hills of South Dakota. It had been given to me by a member of the Sioux tribe with specific instructions about how the pipe was to be made and what rituals were to be used. That particular night was the first time we had used it in an Eagle Clan ceremony.

Each boy was to hold it as he recited an oath to the Clan of the Eagle. As I handed it to the first boy the smoke from the fire moved with it and swirled around the young man's face as he said his oath. This was odd because there still appeared to be no breeze blowing, but no one really took notice until the smoke moved with the pipe as it was handed to the next boy in the circle. The smoke gently caressed his face as he recited the oath and then continued to move with the pipe until the circle was complete and everyone had held the pipe. Then the smoke resumed its upward spiral as if the warrior spirit that had joined us was satisfied with the ceremony.

About a year later another incident happened during a ceremony at a campout in Mississippi. We had taken the troop camping near the historic Natchez Trace and decided to hold an initiation ceremony on the sacred Emerald Mound, a ceremonial mound that had been built by the ancestors of the Natchez Indians sometime between 1250 and 1600. At its base the mound measures 770 feet by 435 feet and is 35 feet high and is indeed an impressive site. No campfires are permitted on the mound so that night, after getting permission from the park ranger to hold the ceremony; I took nothing with me but a flashlight, the peace pipe, and a small CD player with a CD of American Indian music.

My main concern was whether we could get the ceremony in at all. On this particular night it was windy and overcast and the air smelled like there might be a rainstorm brewing. However, our small party of Eagle Clan initiates and members made it through the pitch darkness to the top of the mound and formed our ceremonial circle. It was unusually quiet with no sound except the wind rustling the leaves and branches in the surrounding trees. I turned on the CD and we started the ceremony. Just as we began to pass the pipe there was a break in the thick cloud cover right above us and we were bathed in the soft light of the full moon. At the same moment we heard the screech of an Eagle that sounded like it was circling right above us. This continued until the ceremony was completed and I turned off the CD when it suddenly became pitch dark again, and the sounds of the huge bird stopped. We departed from the mound in reverent silence.

Most people will probably say that all of the events I have described were just coincidences, and that there was nothing supernatural about them. I won't argue with them about it, but they weren't there on those nights. I doubt that they will ever convince the other scouts and leaders who were with me that we were not in the presence of the "Warrior Spirits".

CHAPTER XIV

HAUNTED SPRINGER, NEW MEXICO

Springer, New Mexico is a small town in the northeastern part of the state, an area rich in both history and hauntings. The town was built near the historic Santa Fe Trail and the community was the home of hearty pioneers and cowboys. Some of them are still hanging around according to Melody, a resident of Springer who provided me with information about two haunted locations in the western town.

The first location is the old Brown Hotel downtown. It is now a popular Bed and Breakfast and also boasts an excellent café. Old hotels in western towns often seem to attract spirits as some of my own adventures have proven. This is to be expected since the hotels were usually the center of a community's social life although things could often get rowdy in the old days.

The ghostly activity in the Brown Hotel occurs primarily on the stairs and in a downstairs hallway near the kitchen. Employees and sometimes guests will go into these two areas and are often rudely brushed aside by an unseen intruder who appears to be in a great hurry to go somewhere. Perhaps it is a long gone cowboy late for a poker game or someone running for his life after being caught with an extra Ace up his sleeve. In any case, it is not a very "friendly" ghost.

The other location is the stately old Clegg Mansion, (sometimes referred to as the Mills Mansion after one of its more recent owners). Apparently, old man Clegg who built the mansion was a pretty nasty customer, who even after he sold the mansion, insisted on being taken back there to die. His wish was reluctantly granted and in hindsight that was clearly a mistake because the old fellow seems to be still hanging around.

According to Melody, the house was bought not long ago by a local resident who was trying to restore it to its former glory. The new owner loved the place and his son was handling the renovations for him. Unfortunately, old man Clegg's ghost, who is just as ornery, now as he was in life, did not make the job easy. The tools used by the workers frequently disappeared, and on one occasion when Melody was in the mansion two brooms being used to sweep the stairs mysteriously left the premises.

The brooms could not be found anywhere and had to be replaced. However, either the ghost actually has a sense of humor or just a malicious streak because the two missing brooms showed up again several weeks later. One was in the basement behind a boiler and the other was found under an old pile of brush in the yard. Another incident occurred when Melody's father was talking to the owner's son while the young man was working on the radiator system. He had laid down his screwdriver for a moment to pick up another tool and when he reached for the screwdriver moments later it was gone. It was located later in another room on a window sill.

If the ghost is that of the spiteful Mr. Clegg, he obviously had real problems with efforts to restore his mansion to its original beauty. He seemed to want to keep it as decrepit as he was in his last days when he died there. Then again, maybe he just doesn't like the idea of anyone living there with him.

CHAPTER XV

THE GHOSTS OF KING'S TAVERN: PART 1

An elderly couple sits having a nice dinner in the King's Tavern in historic Natchez, Mississippi. As they are being served their entrees water begins dripping from the ceiling onto their heads. The waitress immediately helps them move to another table only to have water begin dripping on them there too. They are moved again and the dripping water continues to follow them. Finally, the exasperated couple prepares to leave as the owner of the tavern apologizes to them and tries to explain that the water is not the fault of the staff or poor maintenance, it's just that for some reason Madeline doesn't like them.

Madeline is just one of the many ghosts that reside in King's Tavern. The tavern was originally built as an inn for travelers coming down the old Natchez Trace, the major trade route at the time leading to the Deep South. Ricardo King and his wife opened the inn in 1789. Madeline was an indentured servant and was also Ricardo's mistress, a fact that didn't exactly delight Mrs. King when she found out about it. As a result, one night Madeline mysteriously disappeared.

The tavern was sold in 1817 and was eventually used as a private residence. Then in 1930 when some renovation work was being done on the old inn the remains of three bodies were found buried beneath the fireplace hearth in the main room. One of them was the body of a young woman and it was immediately assumed that this was the body of the long missing Madeline, particularly since a jeweled dagger was found near the body. Mrs. King was known to have once had such a dagger.

When the tavern was reopened later as a restaurant staff members began reporting the image of a young woman moving around on the third floor. She was also seen by both employees and patrons in the dining room. She was always dressed in the same homespun dress, and would wander around for a few moments and then vanish.

Madeline was only about sixteen when she disappeared and is still apparently a mischievous teenager. She delights in turning on water faucets all over the restaurant and she hates locked doors. The owners get very tired of being called out in the early morning hours because the alarm system is going off. They will arrive at the building only to find all of the doors unlocked and wide open but the interior of the restaurant is empty and undisturbed.

Madeline loves music and she also loves to harass the restaurant staff. Her favorite trick is to turn up the sound system to maximum volume and when someone turns it down she simply turns it back up again. However, the most bizarre incident occurred one night when the system was blasting even louder than usual to the point that it was ear splitting. Only this time when the employees tried to turn it down the volume control wouldn't work. Finally they gave up and unplugged it but the music continued to blast throughout the restaurant for several hours. The system was checked and rechecked but no explanation could be found for this phenomenon.

The waiting staff has grown used to Madeline's antics. For example, when one of them is carrying a tray of food from the kitchen to the dining room they will sometimes find that the swinging door won't open. They will usually just say something like "cut it out Madeline" and then the door will swing open. They have also gotten used to having ice thrown at them when they are in the kitchen. No one is ever seen throwing the ice; it just comes out of nowhere.

The tavern's young ghost is also very protective of her privacy. The attic is now a room where guests can spend the night, if they dare. This was originally Madeline's room and she doesn't like intruders. Very few guests spend the whole night; they don't like trying to sleep in a shaking bed or having the covers constantly ripped off of their bodies. Madeline also protests any visits to her room by causing various items hung on the walls and rafters of the dining room to start swinging wildly about. This includes such things as old chains and a mallet. In addition, she will cause tables and chairs to vibrate, often when restaurant patrons are sitting in the chairs or trying to eat off of the tables. The King's Tavern is a great place to eat, but it can be disconcerting to have to chase your steak around the table.

The strangest trick ever pulled by this lively spirit occurred some years ago when the attic was being renovated to make it into a bedroom again. The plumber who was putting in bathroom facilities came downstairs in a big hurry and announced to the owner that he was quitting. He claimed it was too dangerous to work up there. When questioned by the owner he finally reluctantly agreed to accompany her back to the room.

He pointed to a pipe protruding from a partially finished wall that was discharging a stream of scalding hot water. It was quickly flooding the room and the owner asked the plumber why he didn't just find the source and turn it off. At that point the exasperated worker told the owner to look behind the wall. The sight that greeted her was beyond comprehension. The other end of the pipe was connected to nothing! There was no apparent source for the water which finally stopped running by itself after Madeline apparently got tired of this particular prank. The rest of the job was later finished by another plumber.

When my wife and I visited the tavern we found the staff eager to talk about Madeline and the other hauntings. We were even shown a scrapbook of various newspaper and magazine articles that have been written about their ghosts. There is also a portrait of Madeline hanging in the foyer. The discovery of the picture was eerie itself. Not long after the tavern was reopened the owner was driving down a Natchez street when she suddenly had an overwhelming urge to turn into the parking lot of an antique store. When she entered the premises she had no idea why she was there or what she was looking for. She walked into a back room and there on a shelf was a small portrait of a young woman in frontier clothing. She knew immediately that this was a portrait of Madeline and that she had to buy it.

When she took it up front to the counter the store's owner was confused to say the least. He had no such picture in his inventory and had never seen it before. He was therefore happy to have the tavern owner take it away. So Madeline's portrait has come home and she continues to both literally and figuratively hang out in King's Tavern. She certainly doesn't reside alone in the historic old inn however.

CHAPTER XVI

THE GHOSTS OF KING'S TAVERN: PART 2

The King's Tavern was at the termination point of the Natchez Trace that in the latter part of the 18th century and early 19th century was the principal trade and travel route from Nashville, Tennessee to Natchez. The Trace was also the home of marauding Indian bands and outlaws of every description. The numerous bullet holes in the front door of the tavern attest to the fact that not all of its visitors were there just for the amenities it offered.

There were killings both inside and outside of the tavern. Aaron Burr stayed at the inn while planning his treason against the newly formed United States of America and there were undoubtedly other conspiracies planned inside the historic building's walls as well. The Natchez Trace itself is now a Federal historical site and a visit to the actual remnants of the Trace often produces an eerie experience. The Trace was so well used that the ground is worn down to a depth of six to eight feet in many places, making the old route a virtual ravine.

As you walk through these portions of the Trace you are surrounded by trees that spread their limbs over the top of the road making it a dark and gloomy place even during the day. It is easy to imagine that there are outlaw or Indian bands hiding in the trees above you waiting to terminate your journey in a hail of arrows or gunfire.

The King's Tavern was the only place for many of the raiders to spend their "earnings" so it is not surprising that some of them and some of their victims would still be hanging around. One of them is seen frequently by both patrons and employees of the inn. He is described as a tall man wearing a red hat and frontier clothing who is seen standing near the bar or by the window. His face is just a blur and there is no way to tell if he was an outlaw or one of the victims of the raiders. Perhaps his body was one of those other two discovered when Madeline's remains were found behind the old fireplace. No one has ever determined their identity or how they got there. The only thing known for sure is that they died violently, as did many other people who frequented the tavern.

Also seen around the tavern is the figure of an Indian. Believe it or not, he is probably the mailman of the time. The first U.S. mail ever delivered to the King's Tavern was brought by an Indian runner from one of the local tribes. He apparently continued to do odd jobs around the place including helping out in the tavern's official U. S. Post office. Unfortunately, the post office was also the site of one of the most infamous murders in the tavern's history. A man called Big Harpe was one of the most notorious and vicious outlaws along the Natchez Trace. He was a regular at the inn and was avoided by everyone because of his well known bad temper. However, on one occasion he was hanging out at the bar, which was also the postal counter, when a young woman from the town came in to pick up her mail.

She had her baby with her in a small basket that she sat down on the floor in front of the bar. The baby boy started crying and despite the mother's efforts to quiet him, he just squalled louder. This irritated Big Harpe to the point that he grabbed the child by the legs and smashed him against a brick wall, crushing the baby's skull and killing him instantly. There was no law in Natchez during that period, so nothing was ever done to Big Harpe.

The sound of a baby's crying is heard all too often around the restaurant, sometimes bringing tears to the eyes of those that know the story. The crying is plaintive and heart wrenching. It usually comes from the area where the old bar is located and nothing is ever found when the area is searched. One can only hope that someday the little fellow's cries will stop and everyone will know that he is finally at peace.

At the time my wife and I visited King's Tavern there were rooms available where you could spend the night but it was not a traditional Bed and Breakfast. If you stay you'll get a great dinner but it is apparently taken for granted that you'll be gone before morning so breakfast is not served.

CHAPTER XVII

THE VOODOO QUEEN

In my ghost hunting I have found that most of the spirits who still walk the earthly realm prefer the comfort of old houses, bustling hotels, or saloons. Yet, it is the cemetery where we mortals most fear to tread, expecting to see one after another emaciated corpse struggling to emerge from their graves, or a ghost waiting in every shadow to burst forth and frighten the unwary.

I've often wondered why this is the case since if I were one of the newly dead, and thoroughly unhappy about the fact, the last place I would want to hang out would be in the cemetery with a bunch of other dead people. In fact, it may be that cemeteries are a good place to avoid ghosts, unless of course you are in New Orleans, Louisiana. That is because they have this major problem in the Crescent City, they can't bury anyone, at least not in the traditional sense.

New Orleans is virtually an island due to the fact that it is surrounded by the Mississippi River, several lakes, and some very desolate swamps. It sits below sea level and as a result if you dig more than three feet into the soil of the Big Easy you hit water. Consequently, the people in New Orleans inter their departed relatives in tombs above ground, literally creating cities of the dead.

The tombs range from simple concrete boxes to ornate structures housing generation after generation of old New Orleans families. It therefore stands to reason that in a city known for its nightlife and parties that it is after dark that the cemeteries become as lively as Bourbon Street, hosting the ghosts of both the famous and the infamous. No graveyard is livelier than St Louis Cemetery # 1 in downtown, and why not, it contains the tomb of the most notorious of the city's former residents, the Voodoo Queen, Marie Laveau.

Her granite tomb is not much different from most of those in the cemetery except for the fact that it is decorated with pleas for assistance, and surrounded by offerings from those residents of the city who believe to this day that while her body may reside in the tomb, her spirit still roams the streets of the Vieux Carre' casting spells for those who are in her favor. During her heyday in the early 19th century Marie Laveau virtually ruled New Orleans. She traded her spells and potions for information, usually from the servants of the rich.

The information she obtained could often destroy marriages and reputations, or bring political careers to an end, so she frequently used what she knew to extort blackmail payments, or favors from the prominent residents of the city. If that did not prove lucrative enough she would offer the information to the highest bidder among the rivals of politicians or businessmen. She was easily the most powerful person in the entire city.

Now, residents tell me that she is often seen roaming the cemetery and the adjacent streets, her illusive figure darting from building to building or tomb to tomb. She will grant favors to her faithful followers, and on occasion will make her presence known in a dramatic fashion. It is often around midnight that locals claim to see a fiery ball of blue light jumping from telephone wire to telephone wire around the cemetery. At first glance it looks like an electrical anomaly, but then suddenly the flaming ball will jump into the dark sky above the cemetery and hover for a moment. Then it slowly descends until it settles on a tomb, that of Marie Laveau, the Voodoo Queen of New Orleans.

There are many frightening stories about voodoo in Louisiana and I have found that it is true that while most spirits do not try to harm anyone there are occasionally ghosts that can be pure evil. I recently heard one such story from a friend of mind named Jeff Neri who is from New Orleans, but he now lives in the Dallas, Texas area and he and his lovely wife Michelle own and operate Dodie's Seafood Restaurant in Carrollton, Texas. It is one of my favorite places to dine and features real New Orleans style seafood as well as a neighborhood New Orleans atmosphere. I highly recommend it to anyone in the area.

During his college years of 1968 -71 Jeff attended Nicholls State University in Thibodaux, Louisiana, which is in the heart of Cajun Country. He stayed in a dormitory on campus his freshman year, but in his sophomore year he got an apartment that he shared with two U.S. Navy veterans who were attending the university. The apartment was directly across from the rear of the largest Catholic Church in Thibodaux.

It was one of three roof top apartments that were on the second story of a building that had stores on the first floor. During the summer Jeff would go back to New Orleans to live because there was where his summer job was. However, he kept the apartment and would sometimes go back to Thibodaux on the weekends. On one such occasion he was in Thibodaux on a Friday night and admittedly had too much to drink so he decided to crash for the night in his apartment. When he went in he stumbled over a sleeping buddy of his who lived in the apartment at the other end of the building.

The young man's name was Bob and he was what Jeff called a bit of a moose. He was a weight lifter who had won power lifting competitions in his home state, but was actually majoring in art at Nicholls State. Jeff didn't think much of Bob's presence and he went to bed. The next morning Bob was still there and as Jeff and his two roommates' were preparing to make breakfast they realized they didn't have enough eggs. One of Jeff's roommates' asked Bob if he had any eggs in his apartment and he said yes, he had plenty of eggs but he insisted that Jeff go with him to get them.

Jeff was very surprised at this since he said that Bob was so strong that he would sometimes jump up on Jeff's bed, grab him by the ankles, lift him up, and swing him like he was just a feather. In other words, the last thing Jeff expected was for Bob to want him along as a bodyguard. Jeff responded by telling Bob he was a big boy and he could carry a dozen eggs by himself, but the young man insisted, and in fact almost pleaded for Jeff to come with him. When Jeff asked his roommates what this was all about one of them said simply that Bob was a little spooked.

When Jeff asked why he was told that Bob's apartment was haunted. Needless to say, Jeff was skeptical at first but everyone insisted that the apartment was haunted and since Bob's roommate was out of town he would not stay in the apartment by himself. Then Jeff realized that this was not some kind of a joke since no one had known he was even in town the night before, much less that he would show up at his apartment to spend the night. Bob was there when Jeff arrived so he was legitimately there to spend the night away from his own place.

Then Jeff heard the story. Bob was dating a self professed witch from New Orleans which probably meant that she was involved at some level with the voodoo culture. He also had a fraternity brother who was a psych major and who liked to do séances and sensitivity sessions. One weekend while Jeff was working in New Orleans the group who lived in the apartments and were all fraternity brothers decided to conduct a séance in Bob's apartment. This happened to be the first time Bob had brought his witch girlfriend in from New Orleans.

When she walked into the apartment she immediately made a comment about the energy in the apartment and she held out her hand a ring flew off of her finger and slammed into a wall as if it had been thrown like a baseball. As they started the séance, they all sat in a circle and they had a human skull with a candle on top of it that they put in the middle of the circle. Jim, who was the fraternity brother that was the psych major, announced that he would be the medium for the séance and he turned the skull that was facing him.

This did not go over well with the witch who told Jim that he was not a medium, she was the medium. Immediately, Bob's cat, that had been sitting in the corner of the room got up and nonchalantly walked over, jumped into the circle and proceeded to nudge the skull until it was facing the witch. There was no more argument about who was the medium.

When the séance moved on things began to fly off of shelves in the room, including some of Bob's artwork that shattered on the floor. This was a good indication that they were dealing with a nasty spirit of some sort and the group should have ended the séance then. However, they continued and the situation quickly deteriorated and got dangerous.

Another member of the fraternity who was in the room was a football player named William. He was a local boy from Thibodaux who was a staunch Catholic who never did drugs as far as anyone knew. Suddenly, William began speaking in a voice that was not his own and was making derogatory and antagonistic comments about the Catholic Church and Christianity. These were certainly not the type of things that William would be saying on his own and everyone in the room was getting very scared. Someone then suggested that they needed to go across the street and get the priest. William's response was to curse the priest.

The people that knew William were aware that he would never say anything like that even as s joke, and would probably have knocked someone down who said such a thing in his presence. The other young men in the room decided that they needed to take their friend to the church immediately and it took all of them in the room to wrestle him to the floor. It was now raining outside and as the fraternity brothers were trying to carry William down the steps he was putting up a fierce fight and they all ended up tumbling down the steps.

William was left with a bad cut on one of his hands and a laceration of his forehead. However, he continued to curse and struggle as his friends carried him across the street and into the church. They manhandled him to the altar and put his hands on it. Immediately, William stopped fighting them, looked around, and in a voice that was clearly recognizable as his own he asked "Why are we in church, and why am I bleeding?" He clearly had no recollection of the events that had just occurred.

Some research was done on the history of the building and it was learned that there may have been some child abuse in the apartment at one time and someone had died in the building. In the meantime, there was still activity in the apartment itself with items being moved and thrown around on their own. The priest was contacted and the story was told to him. He was also asked to do an exorcism of the apartment.

However, it is a long process to get the Catholic Church to approve a full scale exorcism so the priest decided to just come to the apartment to do a blessing. This was done in conjunction with Bob hanging up rosaries and garlic that had been sent to him by his parents when they had heard the story. No one knows exactly what worked, but the activity stopped much to everyone's relief.

There was no indication of voodoo being involved here but there is no doubt that whatever possessed William was evil. The moral of this story is simple. It is not a good idea for amateurs to get involved in séances or use Ouija boards. You never know what you are opening yourself up to.

CHAPTER XVIII

THE MOST HAUNTED CITY IN AMERICA

Of course, Marie Laveau is far from the only ghost that haunts New Orleans which bills itself as the most haunted city in the world. The city does boast one of the most varied histories of any city in the United States. It was originally founded by the Spanish, then taken by the French, and ultimately became part of the United States as a result of the Louisiana Purchase in 1803. Its people are a mixture of many races and cultures, and as a result the superstitions and ghostly tales may come from the creoles, the southwest Louisiana Cajuns, the descendants of slaves brought from Africa or the Caribbean Islands, and the many Irish and Italian immigrants.

When I was growing up in New Orleans I can remember hearing about the hauntings from numerous different sources. Some of the most often told tales concerned the "dueling oaks" in the historic New Orleans City Park. The 100 acre park boasts of some of the most beautiful oak trees in the world, and it was under several of these majestic trees that duels took place in the early 1800s. In fact, during one ten year period there were duels almost every day. The Creole men in the city took their honor seriously and any slight, either real or imagined, could lead them to challenge someone to a duel.

These fights often took place at dawn under the dueling oaks and might involve the use of swords or pistols, and were usually fought to the death. As a result there are numerous stories of people seeing ghostly figures fighting with swords under the City Parks oaks when there is no one there. In addition, visitors to the park may hear several gunshots from the area, but see no one in the vicinity. As a boy I can remember the shiver that went up my spine when I stood under the massive oaks in broad daylight. I just knew that I was not alone and so the thought of coming to the park at night never entered the minds of my friends and I.

The whole area surrounding New Orleans was fascinating for a young boy. There was the mighty Mississippi River where modern versions of old steamboats could still be seen and the mysterious bayous south of the city where the pirates once came to find locations to hide their treasure. A few miles down river from the city is the Chalmette Battlefield where the famous Battle of New Orleans took place in 1814. It was the final and decisive battle of the war of 1812. I can remember wandering through the remnants of the trenches with my Boy Scout troop while the guides treated us to stories of nighttime visitors still hearing the sounds of musket fire, the thundering of cannons, and the mournful cries of the wounded.

The numerically superior and better armed and equipped British army had expected to easily sweep aside the ragtag force of General Andrew Jackson. Jackson's force was made up of a small group of regular army troops, volunteer militia from several states, private citizens of New Orleans, and Captain Jean Lafitte and his pirates. It didn't quite work out that way as the British troops marched straight at the American trenches during their final charge on January 8, 1814. They were slaughtered by the accurate and devastating fire of Jackson's band of men. Over 2,000 British soldiers were killed or wounded while the American forces had only a handful of casualties including 13 dead. I have visited the graves of seven of the dead who are buried together in the St. Louis cemetery, and according to locals at least one of them does not rest easily. A young man in the uniform of a regular Army soldier of that period is often seen wandering about. In fact there are many such sightings on the battlefield itself where the American encampment was. Visitors and employees report seeing groups of soldiers going about their daily routine as if the battle is yet to happen.

There are many areas of New Orleans that attract tourists from all over the world and the most famous is undoubtedly the French Quarter. This area of downtown New Orleans sits along the Mississippi River and is the home to much of the well preserved grand European architecture of the 18th and 19th centuries. Many of these buildings are still homes or apartments, but along famous Bourbon Street and other streets in the Vieux Carre' many of them now house restaurants and bars where some of the world's finest food is available and there is a wide variety of adult entertainment to choose from. A large number of these establishments are reported to be haunted including all of the most famous bars such as Pat O'Brien's, The Old Absinthe House, and O'Flaherty's Irish Channel Pub.

Whenever Kay and I visited New Orleans our favorite spot was always O'Flaherty's where you could hear some of the best Irish music in the world performed by Danny and Patrick O'Flaherty. The pub was located on Toulouse Street and you entered it through an old carriageway that took you to a magnificent courtyard and gift shop. On the right side of the carriageway was the Ballard Room where Danny O'Flaherty performed along with other famous Celtic singers. On the left side was the "Informer" where there was a sports bar with real Irish cuisine for sale and where Patrick O'Flaherty played and sang.

Unfortunately, the pub has been closed since Hurricane Katrina, but there are plans to hopefully reopen it in the future. Until that happens there is no music but you can rest assured that the ghosts are still there. Sightings of several spirits are frequent, including one of a young lady believed to be Angelique who was the mistress of one of the original occupants of the house, Joseph Wheaton. It is said that one night Angelique and Joseph had a terrible fight on the balcony of what is now the upstairs portion of the Ballard Room. At this point the tale varies as to who was pushed or fell off of the balcony. Most people believe it was Angelique, and that shortly thereafter Joseph killed himself in either a fit of remorse or out of fear of being hanged for murder.

In any case, Angelique is often seen on the balcony or in the upstairs rooms and Joseph often appears in the courtyard. There are also very definite cold spots that occur in the courtyard. I experienced these on numerous occasions and believe me when you are in the O'Flaherty's courtyard on a hot summer evening in New Orleans, an encounter with a cold spot can be a heart stopping experience. Kay would often see Angelique and I remember one encounter in particular a number of years ago.

The Kingston Trio, one of our favorite groups, was performing at O'Flaherty's and we went to New Orleans specifically to hear them. During a break in the performance Danny O'Flaherty invited us to come up stairs to the exclusive part of the Ballard Room so we could visit with the members of the trio. We were sitting in the comfortable easy chairs talking to the members of the group about "old times" when I felt a piece of cloth hit me in the side of the face and then slide over my head. I was startled and turned to look to see who might be behind me but there was no one there. I said out loud "What the hell was that?" when I heard Kay laughing. "Don't be so paranoid," she said, "it was just Angelique. I saw her walk by you." Only my Katie would tell me not to be paranoid when I had just been whacked in the head by a ghost.

Joseph and Angelique are not the only spirits who roam the pub. In the Informer there is an old man often seen sitting at the end of the bar. He looks sad and lonely but when spoken to or approached, he simply fades away leaving some patrons wondering if they may have had one pint of Guiness too many. According to local legend he is probably the apparition of an old gentleman who also hung himself in the building sometime in the late eighteen hundreds. Staff members at the pub claim that in addition to occasionally seeing him they also feel his presence throughout the building.

CHAPTER XIX

THE GOVERNOR'S GHOST

As both the Governor of Louisiana and then a United States Senator, Huey Long ruled the state of Louisiana with an iron hand during the 1920s and 1930s. His populist ideas gained national prominence during the depression years to the point that he was becoming a viable candidate for President of the United States. This made many people very nervous and on a hot muggy evening in Baton Rouge in the fall of 1935 Huey Long was met by a hail of gunfire in the main corridor of the new State Capitol.

Allegedly his murderer was Dr. Carl Weiss, but for years most people in Louisiana have known that Dr. Weiss did not actually kill the Governor. The bullets that killed Huey Long probably came from the guns of his own bodyguards who fired wildly that night when they supposedly saw a gun in Weiss's hand. The bullet holes in the marble walls of the State Capital attest to the numerous ricochets that not only resulted in the Governor's death, but in the wounding of several of his bodyguards.

There have also been plenty of conspiracy theories throughout the years laying the real blame for the assassination on everyone from a group of doctors to President Franklin Roosevelt. There is now some doubt as to whether Dr. Weiss even had a gun that night. All of the facts will probably never be known, but one thing that is known is that on his death bed Huey Long's last words were that he wasn't ready to die yet, he had too much left to do.

He apparently meant exactly what he said because he can still be seen stalking the halls of the State Capitol that he had built as a monument to himself. Members of the state legislature and the staffs of these lawmakers have reported seeing him in the visitor's galleries of both the House and the Senate. He is wearing his characteristic white linen suit and watching the events on the floor of the legislature with a critical eye. On at least one occasion he is reported to have confronted a frightened state senator in the hallway, berating him for introducing a bill in the senate that in fact had been offered many years before by one of the Governor's contemporaries. No one is really comfortable in the capitol late at night because you never know when and where Huey will appear and what kind of mood he'll be in.

However, the capitol was not even his favorite hangout in Baton Rouge. In Huey's day during sessions of the legislature much of the actual business was conducted at the Capitol House Hotel, once known as the Heidelberg Hotel. It is in downtown Baton Rouge and for years was closed and abandoned, but has now been renovated to its original grandeur and reopened.

In Huey Long's day the activities at the hotel were often extracurricular and not always related to the political discussions of the day. It is reported that one night a fire broke out in the hotel, causing the evacuation of most members of the legislature and a number of attractive young ladies, all in various stages of dress. No wives of members of the legislature were known to have been present.

Huey Long held court in the hotel in his own luxurious suite. Long after his death frightened hotel maids would refuse to work in the room because, according to them, Mr. Huey was still there. These poor ladies would enter the room and if they were lucky they would only smell the odor of the Governor's expensive cigars. If unlucky they might see him standing by the window surveying his domain, or even sitting in the room's enormous bath tub with a cigar in his mouth, and a stack of proposed legislative bills in his hands.

While the hotel was closed caretakers or security guards would constantly smell cigar smoke throughout the building. Huey never liked being confined to his room and he now apparently roams at will. One sighting occurred before the Hilton Corporation bought the hotel and did the renovations. Another group was considering buying the property and they were doing a survey of the abandoned building. As the group turned the corner in one of the hallways they saw a figure in a white suit, a cigar clamped firmly in his mouth, walking right towards them. They did not have to ask who it was and they promptly vacated the premises.

They should not have worried. Huey was just trying to be helpful. After all he was being very patient in waiting for the hotel to reopen. He's used to the sounds of music and laughter, and he's got business to finish. Now that the stately old hotel is back in business Huey can get back to work.

CHAPTER XX

MYRTLES PLANTATION

It has been labeled the most haunted house in America and from personal experience I can testify that it does its best to live up to its reputation. It is known as Myrtles Plantation and is located in St. Francisville, Louisiana, a small historic community about 35 miles north of the state capitol of Baton Rouge. There have been at least 10 different ghosts allegedly seen in the house or on the property of the plantation which is now a well known bed and breakfast. The most famous and probably the most active spirit is that of a slave named Chloe.

The plantation was originally built in 1796 by David Bradford, a former revolutionary war general who served honorably under General George Washington. However, it has always been rumored that the General was not so honorable when it came to the location of his new home. He built it on top of a sacred Tunica Indian burial ground which may explain some of the hauntings. In 1818 the general passed away and the property was inherited by his daughter Sarah and her husband Judge Clarke Woodruff.

Chloe was one of the house slaves on the plantation and helped take care of the house as well as the Woodruff daughters. Unfortunately, Chloe also liked to spy on the family's activities in the house including the Judge's private business dealings. When she was caught the Judge showed no mercy and had one of Chloe's ears cut off to punish her and warn other slaves who might be inclined to eavesdrop on his private conversations. It seemed never to occur to anyone in the family that Chloe might seek revenge for this disfigurement. She calculated it carefully and decided that the best way to hurt the Judge was to destroy his family. This was done with a poisoned cake on the birthday of one of the daughters she cared for. The cake killed Sarah and two of the girls.

There was no question about Chloe's guilt and the reaction was swift and violent and came not from the Judge, but from the other slaves on the plantation. They took Chloe to a large tree near the house and unceremoniously lynched her. Many visitors to the plantation have reported seeing the spectral figure of her body swaying in the branches of the tall oak tree on windy nights. Others have reported encounters with her in the house itself. For example, guests staying in what was originally her room report their hair being pulled in the middle of the night. Numerous other ghosts are said to roam the grounds since traumatic death seems to have been the order of the day for much of the early history of Myrtles.

My own experience with the spirits at the plantation started off in an innocent enough fashion. I have mentioned that I was the scoutmaster of a large Boy Scout troop in Baton Rouge, Louisiana and we took our scouts on at least one camping trip a month and tried to make each trip a little different from the last one. That's why on a warm September Friday evening in 1993 we had pitched our tents on the grounds of the Myrtles Plantation and were preparing to take the boys to the main house for the ghost tour.

Most of the boys were excited, if a little apprehensive, but they had selected this as a trip they wanted to make. Besides they were used to hearing my wide selection of ghost stories around the campfire. They were treated to the full tour, and heard stories about the origins and sightings of many of the ghosts that are said to inhabit both the plantation buildings and the grounds. After the tour we retired to the campsite and discussed what we had heard. Needless to say it took a while to finally settle the scouts down, but by 11:00 p.m. most of the boys were in their tents and asleep so there were just a few of the older scouts and several adult leaders still up in the camp.

Since everything had calmed down, I decided to take the opportunity to do a little personal exploration of the grounds of the famous plantation. I was particularly interested in the locations where people had experienced encounters with spirits so I made the rounds of these areas. While they were a little spooky in the dark I had no experiences that even hinted at a supernatural presence. At least that was the case until I went to the gazebo.

The beautifully constructed gazebo is located behind the main plantation buildings in a well lit area and is accessed by crossing a bridge over a small pond. Nothing had been said during our tour about supernatural activity in this area, but I decided to visit it anyway since it was on the way back to our campsite. I crossed the bridge and walked in and around the gazebo without experiencing anything and finally decided to call it a night and go back to camp. However, as I crossed the bridge going away from the gazebo I suddenly had an overwhelming feeling that I was not alone on the bridge.

I stopped because I felt a presence behind me and as I started to turn the air surrounding me became very cold and the hair on my arms and the back of my neck stood straight up. This was despite the fact that it was a September night in Louisiana and the temperature was still in the low eighties. It didn't take long to determine that there was no one on the bridge with me or anyone in sight in the immediate area. However, I did not feel like I was alone until I had left the bridge and was almost back to the campsite.

I admit to being slightly shaken but also fascinated and curious about the experience I had just had. This must have been apparent on my face because as I walked into the campsite, David, one of my assistant scoutmasters asked me if I was OK. I told him I was and then invited him to take a walk with me. As we headed back towards the gazebo I told him that I had experienced a strange encounter but gave him no details. We crossed the bridge, looked around the gazebo and then headed back across the bridge without comment. In the middle of the bridge I felt the temperature drop just as I heard David exclaim, "What the hell is that?" I asked him what was wrong and he described the cold area, the feeling of being followed by someone else on the bridge, and his hair standing up, the same things I had experienced. Yet, neither of us saw anyone.

David and I discussed what we had just gone through as we walked back to camp and we apparently aroused the curiosity of several of the older scouts. They asked where we had been and David and I just smiled at each other and told the two boys to go check out the gazebo. Then the two of us sat down by the dying campfire and waited. It didn't take long because within five minutes the two young men came flying back into the campsite like they had been shot from a cannon. They both described the same experiences that David and I had encountered.

The next morning I talked to one of the plantation staff members about the area surrounding the gazebo and what we had experienced. I was informed that during the Civil War there had been a major battle not far from the plantation. Some of the wounded from both sides were brought to Myrtles where a makeshift field hospital had been set up. Some of the men who died had been buried near where the gazebo now was and the ghosts of Confederate soldiers were often seen walking across the pond, which had once been dry ground.

I can't know for sure if these were the spirits that we encountered that night, but there is no doubt that contact was made with some entities that we could feel but not see. This is clearly the reason that the plantation is one of the most investigated haunted locations in the United States. Paranormal investigators always conclude that it is indeed haunted.

CHAPTER XXI

T.J. THE TRAVELING GHOST

When my wife and I visited Cimarron, New Mexico in the summer of 1999 it was to do research for my book **"Riders in the Sky: the Ghosts and Legends of Philmont Scout Ranch"**. We planned on interviewing staff members at the ranch, talking to residents of Cimarron, and visiting haunted sites. What we didn't plan on was bringing one of the ghosts home with us.

I'd heard of traveling ghosts before, but most of the time in reference to spirits who follow a particular family from one house to another. T. J. Wright on the other hand is a different breed of spook. He apparently followed us back to Baton Rouge, Louisiana where we were living at the time, in order to make sure I did right by him in the book.

T.J. was a cowboy who won the famous St. James Hotel in Cimarron in a poker game. He was shot down in the street in front of the hotel by an unknown assailant when he came to claim his winnings the next day, and was taken to room 18 of the hotel where he died several days later. T.J. had won the hotel fair and square and he was not going to give up his rights that easily. He has been in the historic building ever since and has consistently been a rowdy hell raising spirit.

When I did the interviews at the hotel I got the full story of T.J. and the other ghosts that have caused the St. James to be featured in several television shows including the original "Unsolved Mysteries". I took several pictures in the hotel including one of the door to Room 18, the only room in the hotel that can't be rented out, and another picture of a portrait of a Spanish missionary in the lobby. When the pictures were developed the lobby photograph caused considerable astonishment because in addition to the missionary the picture shows a face in the portrait that is not in the original. It is the face of a man screaming and we suspect that it is T.J.

In any event, we returned to our home in Baton Rouge and I immediately started working on the book. Since there are many haunted sites in and around Philmont, it took several months before I got to the chapter on the St. James and its most infamous ghostly resident. That's when it started. As I sat at my desk one night typing the story there were suddenly two loud knocks on the wall behind me. I jumped about a foot and went to check on my wife, Kay, who was in the master bedroom down the hall watching television. She was fine and hadn't heard a thing.

However, the next night when I was in my home office the same thing happened and this time Kay had seen the figure of a cowboy coming down the hallway toward my office. We had a large master bedroom in our home and our chairs in the room faced both the television set and a large dresser next to it with a big mirror. The stairs to the three upstairs bedrooms were right outside our bedroom door and could be seen in the mirror along with the hallway. Kay had clearly seen a tall lanky man come down the steps and head down the hallway toward my office. I never saw him but I heard the banging so we searched the house from top to bottom and found no one.

That same night we began hearing noises from one of the three upstairs bedrooms. They were all vacant because our six children were either out on their own or away in college at the time. The noises consisted of the opening and closing of doors, the sound of footsteps, and banging on the walls. Lady, our cocker spaniel bravely charged up the stairs barking furiously and just as quickly came back down again. She would never go upstairs by herself again.

T.J. became a fixture after that. He was often seen by Kay who on occasion would lose patience with our often noisy companion. I heard her several times yell at him when T.J. was downstairs being particularly disruptive, for example he liked to rearrange items in the kitchen. Kay would shout "T.J. go to your room!" That was usually followed by the clear sound of footsteps going down the hall and then up the stairs, and then the slamming of the door to our oldest daughter's vacant bedroom.

When our youngest daughter was home from college for the holidays she had her own set of problems with T.J. Her bedroom was upstairs next to her sister's former room and T.J. would often be roaming the hall keeping her awake. She reported smelling cigarette smoke although no one in the house smoked cigarettes. I would hear her fuss at the restless cowboy, telling him to "be quiet" and he usually obeyed. Unfortunately, when I occasionally admonished T.J. for something I was casually ignored. Obviously, the ladies of the house intimidated T.J. while I did not.

Of course, we were not sure at first that our new boarder was actually the New Mexico cow hand until I received a phone call from the artist illustrating the Philmont book for me. He was a high school teacher and he told me that while sitting alone in his classroom after school one day he decided to do a drawing of the door to room 18 in the St. James Hotel. Suddenly a picture behind him flew off of the wall and crashed into the wall on the opposite side of the room. Later that night a light fixture fell from the ceiling of his home and shattered at his feet. The artist quickly finished the illustrations and brought them to me.

He was not bothered after that and we never figured out exactly what T.J. disliked about the picture. However, it does show the door to the room slightly ajar and the staff at the hotel said they always kept it closed and locked. Otherwise T.J. would roam up and down the hallway breaking things. We only know that T.J. hung out in our home for about six months and then once the book had been completed and mailed to the publisher he was never seen or heard from again. We can only assume that he was ultimately satisfied with the way I told his story.

CHAPTER XXII

THE GHOST ON INTERSTATE 20

During my time as an amateur ghost hunter I have sensed the presence of ghosts, had physical encounters with them, and even taken pictures of them but I have never felt truly frightened, or even really uneasy. That is until a few years ago when I had a scary encounter in the most unlikely of spots, Interstate Highway 20.

In my travels and studies I have heard and read about ghost ships, planes, and even trains. The most famous of these is probably the Flying Dutchman; the ghost of a magnificent sailing vessel lost in a storm off the Cape of Good Hope and forced to sail there forever, never reaching land.

One legend attributes the curse on the ship to its Captain's use of blasphemous and foul language while another says the Captain is simply engaged in an endless game of dice. Most mariners simply believe that the ship was lost in one of the violent storms that frequent the Cape and its crew continues to sail, looking in vain for a proper burial.

Whatever the origin, there have been numerous sightings over the last two centuries of a sailing vessel with no visible crew on board, its sails tattered and torn, that appears to struggle to reach land, regardless of the direction of the wind. Some sailors have claimed to see a skeleton at the helm of the once proud ship. The ship never responds to attempts to hail it and disappears when approached. Such sightings have been recorded by dutiful Captains in ship's logs for years with no explanation given other than that they had seen the "Flying Dutchman".

I obviously didn't see a ghost ship on I-20, or a plane, or even a train. What I saw, and what disappeared right before my eyes was an eighteen wheel truck. Kay and I had recently moved from our home in Baton Rouge to Dallas, Texas and I had to make several trips back to Louisiana to wrap up some loose ends involving the law practice I was retiring from. I was returning one bright sunny afternoon in May, traveling the last leg of the journey from Shreveport, La. to Dallas. It is about a four hour drive on that stretch but there was not much traffic so I was making good time.

I confess to doing a little in excess of the 70 MPH speed limit and I was slightly annoyed when I came up behind a rather slow moving eighteen wheeler in the right lane. I checked my rear view mirror and saw another car behind me doing about the same speed I was. We both put on our signals and pulled into the left lane so we could pass the truck. I remember glancing at is as I passed and noticing that there were no markings of any kind on either the cab or the trailer which I suppose was rather odd.

I continued on past the truck and again glanced in my mirror to make sure I was far enough ahead of it to safely switch back into the right lane. Much to my shock there was no truck appearing in either my side mirror or my rear view mirror. In fact, the only other vehicle in sight was the white Buick that had been behind me when I started passing the truck.

I was startled and confused, but I didn't panic yet. However, the same could not be said about the driver behind me. I could see him slowing down as I had and he was looking frantically in every direction. He would have been right next to the truck when it abruptly disappeared. I continued to slow down, trying to convince myself that I had imagined the whole thing and I saw the other car pull over on to the shoulder.

I could not go back to him because the next exit was miles away and there had been no exits near us in either direction when this incident occurred. In other words, there was no place for the truck to have pulled off of the Interstate. One minute it was there and the next it was not. I must admit that this time I was badly shaken up. I wasn't expecting to see any kind of a ghost that day, much less that of a truck and driver. At first I regretted not having glanced into the cab at the driver as I passed the truck, but now I'm glad I didn't. I'm not sure I really want to know who or what was driving the big rig that day.

CHAPTER XXIII

THE HAUNTED HISTORY OF SAVANNAH, GEORGIA

The people of Savannah, Georgia readily claim that they live in the most haunted city in the United States. This claim would be vigorously disputed by the people of New Orleans for example, but since I have visited both cities I would have to say that it is a toss-up between the two historic locations. However, in Savannah it is often the case that one's social status is influenced by whether you have a resident ghost in your home or your place of business. Your status is elevated by the very fact that you have a ghost or two residing with you, but it goes even higher up the social ladder if your haunting involves one of the many former Savannah residents or visitors who was an important figure in the history of the city itself, the State of Georgia, or even the United States as a whole.

In order to begin to appreciate how haunted the city actually is you must first become familiar with its history that encompasses elements of unimaginable tragedy and magnificent triumph over adversity. The city was founded in 1733 by British General James Oglethorpe and was to be the first city of the 13th American colony, Georgia. The colony was designed to provide a refuge for the poor of Great Britain so they could start over, and of course raise crops and establish trade that would be beneficial to the British Crown.

However, its primary purpose was to act as a military buffer zone between the other colonies to the north, particularly South Carolina, and the encroachment of the Spanish who were consolidating their hold on Florida and gazing longingly at the British held land to the north. In order to facilitate the defense of the first city of this new colony, Savannah was laid out in a series of squares that provided public areas for business, easily traveled streets, and a location for churches and houses. The squares also provided easily defensible positions. There are still 21 of the original 24 squares left in Savannah and they are carefully preserved.

The people of the city were allowed to worship as they pleased, and that is one of the things that attracted John Wesley to the city in

1736. He would spend much time in the city and would eventually found the Methodist Church. In addition to providing for freedom of religion, General Oglethorpe took another step to help maintain the morality of the people of Savannah. He outlawed what he considered three great evils: slavery, rum, and lawyers. Unfortunately, none of these prohibitions were to last very long.

One of the things Savannah never had to endure was friction with its neighbors and the original inhabitants of the land, the Yamacraw Indians. The chief of the tribe, Tomochichi, became good friends with Oglethorpe and gave him permission to build his city. This friendship endured and Tomochichi's memory continues to be revered by the people of the Savannah. The city grew gradually over the years despite setbacks with some of the agricultural experiments and then in 1778, after the American Revolution had gotten into full swing, the city was captured by the British. In 1779 the Americans, supported by a large French force from the sea tried to recapture the city but suffered devastating losses. The city was actually not freed from English rule until 1782.

After the colonies had gained their independence Savannah began to prosper along with the rest of the state of Georgia. Cotton was king and Savannah was the port where much of the cotton was shipped from. It also became a port where slaves were brought in since the State of Georgia had reversed Oglethorpe's prohibition of slave trade. For the people of the growing southern city the period following the revolution brought both wealth and devastation. Half of the city was destroyed by fire in 1796 and had to be rebuilt. Then the same thing happened in 1820 but it got worse. The city is right on the coast and there is marshland everywhere. The marshes breed mosquitoes and these insects brought yellow fever to the city also in 1820. More than ten percent of the population perished and were buried in mass graves. Other epidemics followed, along with hurricanes and more fires, yet the city survived.

It even survived General William Tecumseh Sherman and his march to the sea during the Civil War. There are two widely told versions of why this happened. Sherman had already burned Atlanta, Georgia to the ground and was intent on doing the same to Savannah. According to most historians the General decided to spare the city the torch because of its beauty. However, many of the people of the city claim that it was spared because of a meeting that took place outside of town between the Mayor of Savannah and the Union Army Commander.

The Mayor is reported to have told Sherman that the people of the city would peacefully surrender and allow the occupation of Union troops if they would not burn it. If that alternative was not acceptable the people of the city would put up one hell of a fight against the advancing Yankees. As an avid student of the Civil War and knowing what I have learned about Sherman, I can't really see him being influenced by aesthetics'. I do know however that his army's ranks were severely depleted by the time it reached Savannah and it was also dangerously short of supplies. Therefore, I subscribe to the second version of the story because I don't believe Sherman wanted another major battle, even with a bunch of civilian militia. Of course, many of the people in the city were of Irish heritage and there is nothing the Irish like better than a good fight, even in a losing cause. I can see why Sherman chose compromise as the better part of valor.

With this type of history it is easy to understand why the city is so haunted. There are ghosts in the houses, the numerous pubs in the city, along the historic riverfront, and in the surrounding battlefields and forts. In fact, the ghosts of Savannah seem to enjoy making their presence known and they are not averse to having their pictures taken. In the next few chapters I will tell you about some of them.

CHAPTER XXIV

THE HAUNTED PUBS OF SAVANNAH

When I arrived in Savannah in April of 2009 to visit my oldest daughter, Michelle, the first thing she did was take me on the famous Savannah Haunted Pub Crawl. This tour is very ably conducted by a U.S. Coast Guard Veteran named Greg Profitt and since I am both a veteran and a ghost hunter we became instant friends. I would highly recommend this tour to anyone going to visit Savannah because Greg knows all about the haunted sites and has had many personal experiences in some of the locations. His stories were backed up by other Savannah residents and my personal research.

One of the first places Greg took us on our tour was to the 17 Hundred 90 Inn. It was originally built in 1790 by a Mr. Powell who owned a shipping business and operated his residence as a boarding house. He lived there with his young bride who he had acquired through New Orleans as an arranged marriage. Powell was an elderly gentleman in his sixties and his bride, Anna was only 12 or 13 years old. Needless to say, this was a loveless marriage and poor Anna was treated no better than a slave by her husband. In addition to her normal wifely duties she was also assigned to handle the paperwork for the ships that her husband had an interest in. These ships sailed in and out of Savannah on a regular basis.

Many of the sailors who came in on ships docking in Savannah were housed at Mr. Powell's boarding house, and it is said that one of these young men fell madly in love with Anna. She felt the same way about him. Since his Uncle was the Captain of his ship plans were made for the young man and Anna to escape when the ship sailed. Unfortunately Anna's abusive husband learned of the plan and locked her in her room. He then ran the sailor off of his property at gunpoint. The ship was forced to sail without Anna but her young lover vowed to come back for her.

Unfortunately, not long thereafter Anna was reported to have committed suicide by throwing herself off of the second story balcony. Greg believes this is not the case; instead he is firmly convinced that

Powell beat her to death and threw her off of the balcony to cover up his crime. Many other people in Savannah share this opinion and so do I. Regardless of how she died, Anna still appears to inhabit room 204 of the Inn. The ground floor is a pub and Anna's room, along with others is available to be rented on the upper floor. People who choose to stay in Anna's room report that she is very fond of jewelry and women's lingerie. These items often disappear from nightstands or luggage. The jewelry usually shows up in another location but the lingerie often stays missing. Anna apparently is collecting a trousseau in case her sailor does come back.

In fact, there are persistent reports that Anna's suitor may be trying to fulfill his promise. Patrons of both the pub and the dining room have reported seeing a young man dressed in a long outdated sailor's uniform roaming the building as if looking for someone. He is seen briefly and then disappears.

In addition to Anna and her sailor there are other spirits who haunt the pub. In his very popular book, "Guide to the Haunted Pubs of Savannah" Greg tells the tale of Kissie, a slave who once ruled the kitchen in the Powell house. She apparently doesn't like anyone else working in her domain, and she has been known to break things or throw items across the kitchen to express her displeasure.

For those who are not afraid to meet the supernatural head on room 204 in the location of Anna's ghost and it is available for rental. However, it is very much in demand so it is a good idea to reserve it well in advance. Be sure to take Greg's ghost tour while there because he has some more great stories to tell about the 17 Hundred 90 Inn.

The next stop on this fascinating walking tour was at WG's Tavern on Lincoln Street. This was also the residence of a couple that was a product of an arranged marriage back in the 19th century between an older man and a teenage girl. However, according to Greg it appears that this arrangement started out as a happy one with the man treating his new bride much better than she had been treated at her previous home. However, within a few years of the marriage the husband's health began to deteriorate since he was already in his fifties, a rather advanced age for the time.

His friends and co-workers became increasingly worried over his growing concern that if he died his young bride would remarry. The man apparently believed that this would keep them from being together in the afterlife and he could not handle that idea. He finally decided that the solution to the problem would be for them to die together so on their fourth wedding anniversary he prepared two glasses of wine containing a strong poison. Greg says that at the last minute he changed his mind and tried to keep his young wife from drinking it. He was too late however, and she quickly died. He turned himself into the authorities who locked him up and went to investigate the scene of the crime. While they were gone the distraught suspect hanged himself in his cell.

This should have been the end to this tragic tale but unfortunately history keeps trying to repeat itself. The original incident had occurred in 1852 and in 1929 there is a young couple living in the same house when the husband began engaging in some very erratic behavior. They both worked at a fish processing plant on the river and after long days the man would go out for a walk and not return for hours. Then one afternoon he disappeared from his job. When his wife got home she found him in their dining room all dressed up with two glasses of wine poured and sitting on the table. Then suddenly he came out of an apparent daze and didn't know what was happening. He didn't know why he was dressed up or where the wine came from.

Of course, things didn't stop there. The husband continued to go out at night and a few weeks later disappeared from work again. This time the young wife came straight home and she found him dead on the floor with a broken glass of wine near him. The authorities found that the second unspilled glass of wine contained poison painted around its rim.

Then it happened again in 1945. The war in Europe had ended and a young American soldier who had landed in Normandy on D-Day, fought all the way through Europe, and survived the Battle of the Bulge came home and married his sweetheart who lived on Tybee Island right outside of Savannah. They moved into the house that is now WG's Tavern. One day the bride came home to find her husband dead on the floor with the inevitable broken wine glass next to him. This time the authorities do a thorough investigation and find poison not only on the rim of the second glass of wine sitting on the table, but on the dead man's lips and the broken pieces of glass on the floor. It appears that the original husband keeps trying to make sure that the man dies first in the new versions of the tragedy.

Greg says that a few years ago a team of parapsychologists investigated the building and without knowing any of the stories found that the building was inhabited by the spirits of a young woman and an older man. The girl often appears in an upstairs window.

The final stop on the Pub Crawl was at the Moon River Brew Pub. The pub occupies the ground floor of what used to be the City Hotel, one of the finest hotels in the old south. It opened in 1819 and attracted not only sailors who came into the city from their ships but also the leaders of Georgia society and the businessmen who bought and sold cotton. The hotel boasted a fine restaurant and bar and was also the place where challenges were made that led to duels by the gentlemen of the time. Dueling was a popular way of settling even minor matters of honor and although it was illegal in Savannah it was easy to cross the river into South Carolina where it was legal.

Once a challenge was made and accepted the seconds for the two antagonists would often meet in the hotel bar to make arrangements for the duel. In fact, many times all of the parties would be present and then leave the hotel to settle the matter. The spirits of the men, who were the losers of the duels, whether dispatched by pistol or sword, would often be seen roaming the hotel even after their demise.

During the Civil War the hotel became a hospital for wounded Confederate troops and it was never reopened as a hotel again. The stately building went through some bad times and in the early 20th century actually became a bordello for a while. There was plenty of action both in and out of the rooms with barroom brawls leading to the ultimate presence of more lost souls roaming the halls of the establishment. Most of the present day activity takes place on the upper floors which are mostly used for storage today. One of the most prominent ghosts is that of a prostitute who was pushed down the stairs after she was caught by a patron emptying his wallet. In fact, Greg reports that she has been seen on occasion falling down the stairs when he has led one of his tour groups to the second floor. It is certainly an attention getter, particularly since she can clearly be seen tumbling down the stairs but immediately disappears when she hits the bottom.

Attempts to renovate the second floor were eventually abandoned and psychics that have been in that area and the floors above have reported the presence of a large number of spirits. Some of these are thought to be pure evil and possibly dangerous. Staff members of the pub and tour guides and members of tour groups have reported being touched or pushed on the second floor. None of that occurred when I was there with Greg, but most of the people that took pictures with digital cameras caught a lot of orbs in their pictures. Such orbs are often associated with the energy of spirits.

There are many other haunted pubs in Savannah and Greg gives details about them in his books: **"Guide to the Haunted Pubs of Savannah"** and **"Scouts Guide to the Ghosts of Savannah"**

CHAPTER XXV

SAVANNAH'S HAUNTED HOUSES

I can't say that all of the houses in the Historic District of downtown Savannah are haunted, but I can say that it is not easy to find one where the residents deny that there is any unusual activity at all. That is certainly the case with some of the more famous locations such as the grand old Owens-Thomas House, the Isaiah Davenport House, and the Sorrel-Weed House. Touring the Owens-Thomas House was fascinating since there is a lot of written documentation about the people who lived there over the years.

The house was completed in 1819 and still stands as one of the finest examples of Regency style architecture in Savannah, or anywhere else. The original owner was Richard Richardson who lost the house after only a few years due to financial setbacks. The home was taken over by Mary Maxwell who operated it as an upscale boarding house. During this period it had its most famous visitor, the Marquis de Lafayette, who visited Savannah after he helped America gain its independence. During the tour we were shown the balcony where this accomplished General gave an address to the people of Savannah. Later the house was acquired by a Georgia Congressman named George Owens. His family and its descendants resided there for 121 years from 1830 until 1951. It was then given by the Congressman's great-granddaughter, Margaret Thomas, to the Telfair Museum of Art. Telfair turned the home into the house-museum that it is today.

After completing the tour I was introduced to a young man named David Casper who works for the Telfair Museum. He is quite up to date on the ghost stories in this part of the city, and we had an interesting conversation. He told me that the most frequent apparition sighted in the Owens-Thomas House is the figure of a man dressed in old style riding attire who moves freely through the house. Perhaps it is the long deceased Congressman who loved this home, or it could be General Lafayette, preparing for a ride in the Georgia countryside. In any case, the figure is seen only momentarily and then disappears. Many of the staff members who work at the house also report hearing eerie noises, and suffering from a feeling of unease and even oppressiveness when working in the carriage house that sits behind the main house. This is not in the least surprising since the carriage house was once the slave quarters for the Owens-Thomas House.

I only had a chance to visit the Isaiah Davenport House briefly, but David informed me that it has at least one rather unusual ghost. It is not a human spirit, but instead the ghost of a tabby cat that has been seen repeatedly for over 100 years. The house is believed to have been built sometime around 1820 and is a marvel to view and visit. However, it is not so great for those who are allergic to cats. Many people who have such allergies have an immediate reaction upon entering the house although there has not been a cat in residence for many years, at least not a mortal one. The house is now run as a house-museum by the Telfair Museum and David Casper told me that many of his fellow employees have seen the cat in the building. However, if you visit the house and don't see him, don't despair, you can apparently buy a stuffed likeness of him in the gift shop.

Of course, no pet should be left alone to haunt a house. As a result, the apparition of a young girl has been seen on the top floor playing with a ball. She may very well be waiting for her cat to come join in the game. An apparition has also been seen in what is now the gift shop and it may be the same little girl, or perhaps it is another former resident trying to track down a wayward pet.

If you are visiting Savannah you must go to the Sorrel-Weed House where you can get not only a wonderful historic tour of this famous house, but also a ghost tour of one of the most investigated haunted houses in the area. The house was built on Madison Square in 1840; however the site where it was located already had its own macabre history. During the siege of Savannah in 1779 American and Allied troops occupied trenches where the home is currently located. When they prepared to make an attack their artillery opened up and was supposed to clear the way for the charge. Unfortunately, the American artillery fire fell short and devastated its own troops. Thus the site of the Sorrel-Weed House was cursed ground from the beginning.

Our tour of the house was conducted by a very talented young woman named Michelle Stonge. Since we were the only ones on the tour at that particular time I was able to question her extensively about the site. She took us to the basement of the house where the slaves used to prepare the meals for the family. It is important to note that this area and the rest of the property have been thoroughly examined by several professional groups who use modern technology to investigate so called paranormal activities. One of these is the TAPS team from the Science Fiction Channel on Cable Television. This particular group has always impressed me because they approach each site as skeptics, and plan to debunk the ghost stories by finding rational explanations for the phenomena. In the case of the Sorrel-Weed House this didn't work. They found too much evidence of true paranormal activity.

For example, their infrared cameras saw the imprints of handprints on one of the walls in the basement. Since such heat imprints don't last for long they had to have occurred during the time the team was in the room, and there was no mortal person who could have caused them. I took a number of pictures while in this location and although I got no handprints I did get some of the unexplained orbs that many people attribute to signs of spirit manifestations. However, the best was yet to come.

Michelle took us to the carriage house which is in the process of being converted to a gift shop. The upstairs was the original home of a slave girl named Molly who was the secret lover of Francis Sorrel, the master of the house. When Francis's wife Matilda came looking for him at one point to help her plan a party she found him in an intimate embrace with Molly in her quarters. This revelation was more than she could handle and she rushed back up to the second floor of the house and threw herself off of the balcony. She died instantly. To this day there are often unexplained cold spots in the courtyard where Matilda died. These occur even in the heat of a Savannah summer.

Francis was devastated by his wife's death and he locked himself in his room to grieve. This lasted for several weeks and then he felt compelled to visit Molly again for comfort. Unfortunately for him, he found that Molly was quite dead, hanging from a rafter in her room. The Savannah authorities at the time labeled it as an obvious suicide but according to Michelle, documents found in the house years later told a different story. The sons of Matilda and Francis had blamed Molly entirely for their mother's death and had arranged for her murder.

This seems to have been confirmed a few years ago by some professional ghost hunters who set up recording devices in Molly's room that actually recorded the voice of a woman screaming the words " Help, get out of here, Oh my God, Oh my God." This is believed to be Molly yelling at her attackers before they hanged her from the rafter. When Michelle let me go upstairs in the carriage house to Molly's room she told me that one thing they wondered about was where exactly in the room the hanging had occurred? As I walked through the room and took pictures I immediately felt a very cold spot in the far right hand corner of the room. I may be wrong, but I believe that is the spot where poor Molly died.

After we finished the tour I had an opportunity to meet with John, one of the investors of the Sorrel-Weed house and he had his own stories to tell about the place. He lives in Atlanta and frequently comes down to Savannah to spend a few days in the house. He stays in one of the first rooms that was renovated and was told by mediums that the work done in such rooms is often upsetting to the spirits. The second night he spent in this particular room he awoke in the middle of the night with the mattress of his bed being depressed all around him. He then felt his chest being constricted like he was being smothered.

Shortly after this experience they had some paranormal investigators in the house from the Port Orange Paranormal Society who spent the night and recorded a lot of activity in that room including a voice saying "what are you doing here? Get out!" Since his initial experience in the room John also reports that he wakes up every morning at 3:00 am for no apparent reason and can't go back to sleep for sometimes two or three hours. Even when he takes Tylenol PM he can rarely avoid this wake up call. The group from Port Orange came back a second time to attempt to help the spirits in the house move on, but the results have been mixed so far.

Orb floating in front of the fireplace in the old basement kitchen of the Sorrel-Weed house in Savannah

Rafter in room in carriage house of Sorrel-Weed house where Molly was hanged

Wall in the Sorrel-Weed house in Savannah where the TAPS paranormal investigation team
of the Scifi channel picked up handprints with their infrared equipment
when no one else was in the house

CHAPTER XXVI

SAVANNAH'S HAUNTED SQUARES

If you tour the historic squares in Savannah you will hear ghost stories about many of them. One of the stories I heard repeatedly from many different sources concerned Wright Square. It is a story about an indentured servant from Ireland named Alice Riley who was bound in 1733 to serve a rather nasty character named William Wise. While serving Wise Alice fell in love with a young man in Savannah. There is some confusion among historians about who this man was, but what happened to him is a fact. In any case, Wise had a habit of mistreating his servants, and required Alice to groom him every day by bathing him and washing his hair. She quickly grew tired of this unsavory duty and his constant sexual advances.

Finally, in 1734 she had suffered enough of the indignities imposed on her by Wise and she apparently murdered him by using his neckerchief to strangle him while holding his head underwater in the bucket where she washed his hair. However, there is also some confusion here because I also heard that she slashed his throat while shaving him. In any event, the deed was done and Alice, with the help of her lover, attempted to flee Savannah but they were soon apprehended by the authorities. They were tried at the courthouse on Wright Square for the murder of William Wise, found guilty, and both sentenced to death. Alice asked for mercy from the Judge because she claimed to be pregnant, which in fact she was. Whether the child was that of her boyfriend or William Wise remains unknown, but in any case the Judge delayed the hanging until the child was born.

Eventually both of the convicted murderers were hanged from a tree in Wright Square, and the child was reported to have died shortly thereafter. Many of the people of Savannah still consider this to have been an unjust hanging and claim that Alice cursed the square just before she died. The fact is that most of the trees in the city are covered with Spanish moss. Yet, that is not the case in Wright Square. I visited the corner of the square where the executions occurred and the local inhabitants are correct. It is one of the few locations in the city where there is no Spanish moss on the trees. It is present on the other trees in the square, but not where the hanging occurred.

In addition, I was told by another tour guide, Bill, that there have been reports of frantic phone calls made to the police department by visitors to the square who describe a young woman wearing ancient clothing who is roaming the square asking for help in finding her missing child. However, she vanishes before the police arrive. Many people think that this is the restless spirit of Alice Riley searching for the child she never got to nurture.

There is also another square in Savannah where the Spanish moss refuses to grow. This is Greene Square that is named in honor of General Nathanial Greene who was second in command to George Washington during the American Revolution. He lived in Savannah following the war, and was reported to have been collecting Spanish moss one day. It was often used for the stuffing of mattresses, but to this day people are warned not to pick it up because it is often infested with various insects, particularly red bugs. Greene apparently received numerous bites from these nasty fellows and became ill.

Thereafter, he hated the moss and ordered his slaves to gather and burn any of it that was near his home. He personally supervised this operation and that was not a good idea for someone of his age during the heat of the Savannah summer. He ultimately died from what was suspected to have been a heat stroke. However, his quest against the moss did not end there. There is no Spanish moss growing in Greene Square, despite the fact that this is virtually impossible in a southern city like Savannah. The moss spreads from tree to tree when the spores are blown by the wind and all of the surrounding squares contain the moss. Yet, while the same spores must be blown into Greene Square, it remains moss free.

Hanging tree in Wright Square in Savannah where Alice Riley was hanged and no Spanish moss has grown on this tree since that time

CHAPTER XXVII

SAVANNAH'S HAUNTED GRAVEYARDS

There are several historic cemeteries in Savannah and I visited two of the most famous while I was there. Yet, many of the locals claim that the city itself is constructed on the site of one mass graveyard. There is a great deal of truth to this. When Oglethorpe laid out his plan for a colonial city built of squares he planned for them to be surrounded by businesses, homes, and churches. However, he did not include enough land in the plans for the churches to have cemeteries. As a result, people were usually buried near where they died, whether that was outside of their homes, in a mass grave on a battlefield, or in the case of yellow fever victims, in mass graves at the nearest available location.

This has led to serious problems for the city as it expanded and modernized. When sites were being prepared for the construction of new buildings it often had to be halted when human remains were uncovered during the excavation of the land for foundations. Since many of these remains are unidentified and now disturbed, it represents just cause for restless spirits to inhabit these areas. One of the most notable sites is the Savannah Visitors Center. This is a beautiful structure where most of the historic and ghost tours of the city originate. The center is by the old railroad yard and is virtually built on top of the mass grave of the 1100 Colonial troops who were killed in the space of less than an hour when they charged the British positions during the American Revolution. These soldiers were met with unexpected resistance including massed cannon and musket fire from well prepared English fortifications. It is reported that following the battle the American forces were given a short period of time by the British to collect their wounded and bury their dead. This caused a decision to be made to place many of the mortally wounded soldiers who were considered beyond help into the mass grave with the already dead. In other words, some soldiers were buried alive.

This has resulted in numerous accounts by staff members and patrons in the visitor's center of glimpses of men in the uniforms of Colonial soldiers roaming through the building. They are usually seen for just a few seconds before they disappear, and visitors often ask if there is a reenactment of the battle being staged that day. The answer is always no, these are not people in costume; they are the spirits of soldiers who died there. It is also reported that on the anniversary of the battle, October 9th, there is another unexplained phenomena. Outside of the Visitor's Center there is a field where a large number of stones are placed as a monument to the brave men who died there. Many of the stones are marked with the names of the fallen. In the early morning of the yearly anniversary of the ill-fated assault many Savannah residents have reported seeing dancing lights on the stones. No explanation has been found for this so it must be concluded that the spirits of the fallen are making their presence known so they will not be forgotten.

I believe that any visit to Savannah must include tours of the historic Colonial Park Cemetery and the Bonaventure Cemetery. The Colonial Park Cemetery was the first real graveyard established in the city in 1750. It accepted the dead of Savannah for a little over a century. Yet of the approximately 11,000 people buried there only about 600 have gravestones that mark their passing. Many of the others lie in mass graves and are the victims of yellow fever, fire, or the other tragedies that have marred the city's history.

Unfortunately, even many of these few grave markers are inaccurate. When General Sherman and his Union army occupied the city his cavalry was assigned to bivouac in the Colonial Park Cemetery. It was the dead of winter and the first priority of the Yankee horsemen was to stay warm. This meant moving into many of the brick family vaults that are present throughout the cemetery. Some of these vaults contained generations of deceased family members either residing in coffins in niches in the walls or is some cases just in decaying burial shrouds.

The troopers were not particularly willing to share their new quarters with the remains of people who no longer needed to worry about keeping warm so they unceremoniously tossed the bodies out of the crypts. It is safe to assume that many of the coffins were broken up to be used as firewood and the bones they contained probably dumped in untidy piles. This means that when the Yankees finally left and the families tried to re-inter their loved ones, they were unsure who belonged to which crypt. As a result Aunt Mary's skull might now be occupying a newer coffin with the ribs of a male neighbor that she never particularly liked. Of course, this provides even more reason for the spirits of Colonial Park Cemetery to be unsettled.

If that wasn't enough, the union soldiers also quickly got bored during their occupation of Savannah. There was little for them to do when they were on duty so some of them amused themselves by altering some of the tombstones in the graveyard. This resulted in such interesting grave markers as that of Josiah Muir who has a marker showing that he died at age eleven, but was survived by his 17 year old wife, and his twelve year old son. Other markers in the cemetery indicate that residents of Savannah lived to ripe old ages of up to 1,491 and in one case even 1700 years of age. Of course, I always heard that sea air is good for you. However, I believe that if I was a citizen of Savannah that had been peacefully interred in the cemetery for years only to have my rest disturbed by a bunch of "Damn Yankees," I would be one restless spirit from then on.

I visited Colonial Park Cemetery twice during my short stay in Savannah. Once was during the day when I got to see the altered markers and visit the graves of some of the more famous citizens of the historic city including Button Gwinnett who was one of the signers of the Declaration of Independence. A wide variety of Savannah residents now inhabit this site, from heroes of the American Revolution to those who were the losers in duels between gentlemen. There are graves of genteel ladies of fine southern families, and those of the lower rungs of society who may have died in a yellow fever epidemic resting right alongside of the fashionable ladies.

My other visit to the graveyard was at night, but unfortunately I could not go inside the cemetery gates. In late 1999 and early 2000 the remains of several sacrificed goats were found in the cemetery. It is not known whether these were the result of bizarre pranks, or some actual demonic ritual, but authorities decided to lock the cemetery gates at night to keep people out. As a result, I was relegated to walking the perimeter of the cemetery outside of the fence and taking pictures. One of these photos proved to be very interesting since it contains a rather large orb in front of a gravestone in the cemetery. Perhaps it is one of the inhabitants of the old graveyard reminding me that there is still some activity on the site, or perhaps not. Either way, it can't come close to what happened to me a few days later in another famous Savannah Cemetery.

Bonaventure Cemetery is on the outskirts of Savannah and is by far the most beautiful cemetery I have ever seen. It is spread out over a large area with great oak trees everywhere that are covered in Spanish moss. It is also adorned by numerous Azalea bushes and other foliage that makes it seem more like a garden spot than a place where the dead rest. It was officially established in 1869 and contains the bodies of not only many former soldiers who fought for the Confederacy but also those Savannah residents who fought valiantly in the later wars to protect the freedom of Americans. There are also the graves of many other notable Americans including the great songwriter, Johnny Mercer who wrote such classics as "Moon River".

The most commonly seen spectral visitor in the graveyard is that of a man in a Confederate army uniform who walks through the area. I didn't see him, or any other vision of a ghost that day, but what occurred is no less remarkable. My daughter, Michelle, drove me to the cemetery, but she stayed in the car as I got out and walked around. I saw a few other visitors to Bonaventure while I was there, but they were always far away from me. Since there were no sounds around but those that nature provided I decided to conduct an EVP session while I was there.

I had no map of the cemetery and no idea of who was buried there. I was walking aimlessly and when I found an interesting grave or group of graves I would record it and then tell any possible spirits that if they wanted to speak to me, now was the time to do so. I would leave the recorder on for a while and then move on. When I was walking with the tape recorder running you can clearly hear the sound of my footsteps since I was walking on gravel mixed with fallen tree limbs and dried leaves. Nothing else is heard until I stopped at the burial site of a father and son who had served in the army during the Spanish American war. I thanked them for their service to our country and then asked if they had anything to tell me. I waited for a minute and then began to walk again with no clear idea of where I was going next.

Later, when I played the tape I didn't hear any voices, but I heard something just as strange. The sound of my lone footsteps is clear on the recording and then suddenly you can hear an additional set of footsteps with mine. Then there is another set of footsteps and another until suddenly there is the clear sound of many men marching in perfect cadence. I am a U.S. Army veteran and I know this sound but I didn't trust my own senses so I played the recording for members of my American Legion Post. Some of them reported hearing the sounds of at least a platoon of marching men while others contended that it was no less than a full company.

The recording ends when I stop once more and announce that I am at the site of the American Legion section of Bonaventure Cemetery where the bodies of the Savannah veterans of World War I and World War II are buried. I have no doubt that on this particular journey through the cemetery I was accompanied by a group of American heroes who had given their all for our country. I was both humbled and honored by their presence with me that day.

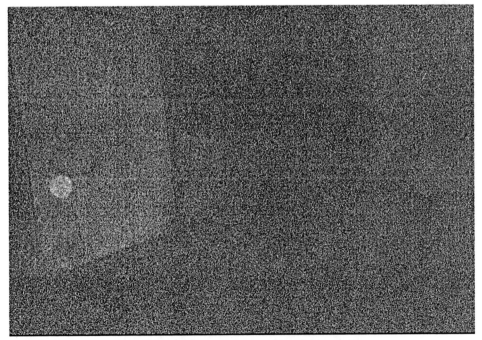

Orb floating in front of a gravestone in
Savannah's Colonial Park Cemetery

CHAPTER XXVIII

OTHER SAVANNAH SPIRITS

Savannah is in many respects a military town. Hunter Army Airfield is located in Savannah and during World War II the legendary 8th Air Force was formed in Savannah. Its members flew hundreds of missions against the Germans in Europe and there is now a wonderful museum in the city honoring these airmen. It is well worth visiting. There are also some historic forts in the area and on the second day of my visit we went to Fort Pulaski that is named for Count Casimir Pulaski, the General who died while leading French and American troops in the ill-fated attack on the British garrison in Savannah in 1779. The fort was built on the site of several previous forts and was occupied by United States troops until it was seized by Southern militia prior to the start of the Civil War.

Its solid brick construction was thought to be impenetrable by cannon fire but no one had considered the possibility of rifled cannon being deployed by union troops stationed on nearby Tybee Island in 1862. The walls of the fort were quickly breached and the confederate forces inside were forced to surrender. I walked around the outside of the fort and it was indeed an eerie feeling to look at the areas where the walls had been breached and the places where you can clearly see the cannon balls buried in the masonry. If it had not been for this battering by artillery fire it would have been very difficult for union troops to take the fort with an infantry assault. Fort Pulaski is surrounded by a deep moat and anyone attempting to swim across it would have had to contend not only with rifle fire from the parapets of the fort, but with the alligators who occupied the murky water.

During our visit to the historic fort my daughter and I were accompanied by old friends from Louisiana, Rhett and Judy Bunch and their daughter Lauren. Rhett is a highly regarded Cajun cook and has a following even in Clemson, South Carolina, where he and Judy now live. As we walked around the fort we saw a large alligator lounging on top of the water. We stopped and quickly agreed to name him Boudreaux. We then started to talk about what a fine specimen he was and how his meat could be used for some great fried alligator and a wonderful Alligator Sauce Piquant, a renowned Cajun dish. We are convinced that Boudreaux understood every word we said because he opened his eyes, rolled them up in our direction and gave us a look that clearly said, "These people are crazy and they will eat me." He then submerged and proceeded to put as much distance between him and us as he could.

When you consider the fact that Boudreaux's ancestors occupied this moat during the Civil War it is surprising that any of the confederate prisoners incarcerated there after the Union soldiers took the fort even tried to escape. Yet some did, but were unsuccessful, although none fell prey to the reptile population. The brutality of the incarceration of these southern soldiers led them to take desperate measures. By 1864 union troops had become aware of the deplorable conditions that existed for Union prisoners of war who were housed in Andersonville Prison in Sumter County, Georgia. Thousands of men who wore the blue of the United States Army died there as a result of disease and malnutrition. Their brothers in the Union army decided to retaliate by giving similar treatment to the confederate prisoners then housed at Fort Pulaski.

This unfortunate group became known as the Immortal 600, a band of Confederate Officers who were incarcerated during the brutal winter months of 1864 to 1865. They lived in unheated casements and often survived on the rats or other vermin they could catch. Many died and are buried in unmarked graves in the fort's cemetery. It is not surprising that the fort is haunted. When I entered the areas of the fort where these men had tried to cling to life, I was almost overwhelmed by a feeling of despair. The suffering they endured hangs in the air like an oppressive cloud. People who are sensitive to the spirits that inhabit some locations often have to immediately leave the area and the ghostly figures of confederate soldiers are often seen in the compound.

In addition, the specter of a Chaplain who served both the Confederate prisoners at Fort Pulaski and the Union soldiers incarcerated at Andersonville is sometimes encountered. He seems to be still trying to ease the suffering of all of these brave men regardless of whether they wore blue or grey.

The Telfair Mansion was designed by one of America's earliest and most famous architects, William Jay and was constructed in 1818. It served as the family home until the last member of the family, Mary Telfair, died in 1875. She and her sister Margaret wanted the home turned into a museum and Mary also endowed the Historical society with other property and funds to maintain several historic sites in the city. Unfortunately, Mary and Margaret had a somewhat troubled history and most staff members of the museum believe that Mary still makes her presence known, even today.

According to the story I heard from several different sources, Mary and Margaret both fell in love with the same man in their younger days when they were traveling in Paris, France. Margaret was the younger of the sisters and by far the most attractive and she eventually won the young man's heart. They were married and this did not sit well with Mary. I imagine the situation didn't get any better when all three of them ended up living in the mansion in Savannah. However, somehow Mary endured it although she apparently never recovered from her broken heart and developed a complete dislike for all members of the male gender. Margaret's husband, William Brown Hodgson, was the first of the trio to die, and so Margaret expressed her desire to have the property turned into a museum when she died. After Margaret died Mary also wanted the property preserved but she put some severe restrictions on the legacy in her will. In the museum there was to be nothing that constituted an amusement and this included strict prohibitions against smoking, drinking, and eating.

These restrictions included another structure called Hodgson's Hall that was under construction at the time both Margaret and Mary died. These prohibitions were strictly adhered to until the Historical Society began to run out of money to maintain the facilities and it became necessary to hold fundraisers to replenish the funds. Unfortunately, the initial fundraising efforts were disastrous failures. Since food, drink, and other amusements were provided Mary would get quite upset. Things would happen like Mary's portrait falling off of the wall, lights going out, and tables of refreshments collapsing.

Even an attempt to hold a fundraiser outdoors in the square the mansion sits on failed when a sudden storm blew up with high winds and rain. When the festivities were moved into the mansion all hell broke loose and the event was ultimately cancelled. It is interesting to note that

I was told that according to both eyewitnesses and the weather service, the storm was only confined to that square and there was no wind or rain anywhere else in Savannah that day. Finally, the staff threw in the towel and eventually fundraisers were held in other locations such as the newly constructed annex. However, Mary's presence is still felt in the mansion and she is reported to get very irritated if anyone tries to relocate her portrait from its rightful place in the dining room. One such attempt was met with part of the ceiling collapsing around a new location. The portrait was quickly moved back to its original place of honor.

The Pirate's House Restaurant in Savannah was certainly one of the most interesting places I visited. There is a lot of dispute about when the original building was constructed with some people claiming it was built in the mid 1700s while others say it was in the later period of the same century. What is known is that it was a tavern frequented by sailors who served on ships docked in Savannah and this included privateers. Privateers were not technically pirates because they served on ships that were given Letters of Marque by a government that authorized them to attack and capture the merchant ships of rival nations. These were issued not only by various European countries, but also by the newly formed United States Government.

The privateers were allowed to sell the ships and cargo they captured and the money was divided among the crew. It could be a very lucrative business, but it was also often a brutal one. It was widely known that crews of captured ships were sometimes put to death and this meant that the crews of the ships under attack often put up a fierce fight before they were overcome. Being a privateer was a dangerous job and many men were lost. Volunteers were not always easy to find and so other sailors or even unsuspecting men off the streets were shanghaied to replace the losses suffered by some ships.

Savannah was a busy port, but not very hospitable to privateers or other sailors. This was primarily due to the fact that no alcohol was allowed in the city and this was not a situation that men who made their living on the sea were accustomed to. This problem was quickly resolved because the original Pirate's House was so close to the river. Privateers dug a tunnel from the basement of the would-be tavern to the river and brought in their own kegs of rum. They also quickly learned that this tunnel was a good way to smuggle shanghaied men out to their ships where they could be chained below decks until the privateers set sail.

Men who were passed out from the drinking of too much rum were easy prey, but those that were awake and reasonably sober often put up a fight and many of them were unceremoniously thrown down the steps into the rum cellar. If they were just rendered unconscious and suffered no more than cuts or bruises they were quickly hustled to the ships. However, some died immediately from broken necks and others suffered broken bones that made them useless for shipboard duty. They were finished off and their bodies dumped in the river. It is no wonder that the rum cellar of the Pirate's House, and in fact, the whole building is a hotbed of ghostly activity.

For a while the upstairs was occupied by a Jazz bar named Hard-Hearted Hannah's and items were often thrown about by unseen hands, including coffee pots which were broken against walls or on the floor. During that time, and since the site became a restaurant, staff members and patrons have reported seeing sailors in old time costume walking around the premises, often disappearing when they walk through the walls. Some have even claimed to have seen the ghost of the most famous privateer of them all, Jean Lafitte whose ships frequently visited Savannah. He was originally a privateer operating under a Letter of Marque issued by the British allowing him to prey on French ships in the Caribbean and the Gulf of Mexico. However, he is best known for supplying the cannon, shot, gunpowder, and men to General Andrew Jackson that helped the future American President destroy the British army that tried to capture New Orleans in 1814.

If you enter the rum cellar in the Pirate's House on a tour you will find yourself in a brick lined room that is not very large, but which was the original entrance to the now sealed tunnel to the river. Some people report being touched by an unseen presence in the room but this didn't happen to me. What did occur was even stranger. I took numerous pictures with my standard 35mm camera. When I developed the pictures there was one that showed a large number of orbs of various sizes hovering around the ceiling of the building. There was another picture that was even more remarkable. It was the photograph of a full body apparition of a young woman wearing the clothing that would have been prevalent in the late 18th and early 19th Century. She also has the typical hairdo of the time.

I later learned that there is a story of a young woman who worked in the tavern who either fell or was pushed down the steps of the rum cellar and died there. What made the picture stand out even more is the fact that my daughter Michelle took a separate picture in the same location with her digital camera. She got exactly the same image that I did. This is highly unusual and confirms that there was somebody in the cellar that night that was not part of the tour.

Orbs along the ceiling of the old rum cellar of the Pirate's House restaurant in Savannah

Photo of full body apparition of a woman in a period clothing taken in the old rum cellar of the Pirate's House restaurant in Savannah

CHAPTER XXIX

GHOSTS OF THE TEXAS HILL COUNTRY

To the west of San Antonio, Texas lies one of the most majestic areas of the Lone Star State, the Texas Hill Country. The history of the area provides a fertile breeding ground for ghosts. There were frequent clashes between settlers and the Indian populations that ultimately led to the construction of U.S. Army Posts throughout the region. Many of these forts were built prior to the Civil War and were eventually occupied by Confederate troops, but later retaken by Union soldiers. Of course, the famed Texas Rangers were also added into the mix.

My headquarters for my stay in the area was at Bandera, Texas, a town of less than a thousand people that advertises itself as the "Cowboy Capital of the World". In fact, for many years the town was the starting point for numerous cattle drives that took the prized Texas Longhorn cattle to distant towns where they could be sold and then transported by railroad to their ultimate destination.

Not far from Bandera is the site of Camp Verde, a historic cavalry outpost where a unique experiment was conducted. The post was established in 1855 and the U.S. Army decided to import a number of camels into the area for use by the troopers. It was believed that these camels from the African deserts would be perfectly suited to the arid climate of the Hill Country since they could travel for long distances with little water. Unfortunately, the experiment proved to be a spectacular failure. The camels were accustomed to walking in the sands of places like the Sahara Desert. Their hooves could not adapt to the rocky terrain of the Texas landscape, and they soon became lame. The whole idea was eventually abandoned as was the outpost after being seized by Confederate troops during the Civil War and then reoccupied by Union troops in 1865.

The original camp has fallen into ruin and most of the land is privately owned. However, on the edge of the area the post once occupied is the Camp Verde General Store which was originally a large home and store built on the site to service the troopers at the camp. There are several active spirits here, one in the store and another outside. There is a beautiful creek outside of the store which is crossed by a bridge on the adjacent highway. However, in the mid 1800s there was no bridge and the creek had to be crossed either in a wagon, on horseback, or by foot. This was usually safe enough unless there had been heavy rain in the area, and then flash flooding could cause the crossing to be very dangerous indeed. According to local legend, during the Civil War a Texas Confederate soldier was going home on leave and was anxious to see his lady love that lived near Bandera. He tried to cross the creek when it was flooding and was drowned. He is often reported to be seen to this day, trying in vain to make the crossing.

Inside the General Store there is a ghost that everyone calls Ruthie. She is reported to be a very active spirit who frequently moves things around in the store and on one occasion actually took a framed painting off of the wall and threw it at one of the employees. Ruthie does not like men and does not allow them to go into the basement of the building. The story is that the house was purchased many years ago by a man who would capture local girls from the Indian tribes and keep them in the basement to be sold as slaves. Ruthie is believed to be the spirit of one of these young women, perhaps one of the captives who died in the location before being sold.

The store is now owned by a corporation and I was not allowed in the basement without permission from the company, but I did go upstairs in the gift shop where Ruthie is also supposed to be active. Using a digital camera I got photos of an orb around the ceiling that could very well be Ruthie manifesting herself. With the help of friends, I used several methods to block out the light from any sources that might be causing reflections that could account for this orb. Despite our efforts over a period of approximately a half hour, the orb was still present. Therefore, it was clearly not a speck of dust that would have fallen away during the investigation.

Some very interesting other things happened when I was in the Camp Verde General Store and people found out I was a ghost hunter. They started to come forward with other stories from other areas. One of these people was Tink Nathan who is a documentary film producer and he told me about a ranch started in 1899 near Camp Verde that had a haunted building that may have ultimately been burned down because of all of the hauntings. The building was at one time a bunkhouse for Mexican laborers on Texas Highway 41. A number of things have happened in this building including the sounds of chains going up and down the stairs. Bow hunters used to frequent the camp during the hunting season and in the morning the tables would be cleaned and set despite the fact that the night before the tables had been covered with beer cans and trash. They thought the ranchers had set the tables. This was not the case. There was also a door that would be impossible to open despite the fact that it could not be locked and usually opened easily. Hunters would hear people walking around when no one was present and there were other mysterious noises that ultimately caused the group to stop coming on the property.

I also met a delightful lady named Janet Dunbar who lived in a haunted house in Gatesville, Texas which is south of Dallas near the city of Waco. They had rented a house and had lived there for about five years. During that time Janet and her mother and sister, who occupied the home, would often go to sleep and then abruptly wake up to see a large man wearing a black suit standing by their beds. They all had separate bedrooms and never discussed their encounters with the phantom gentleman until some ten years later when they had been away from the property for quite a while. Then they discovered that they had all been seeing the same vision and they were all aware that a man had once died in the house.

In the historic town of Fredericksburg, Texas there is a site where the U.S. Army established Fort Martin Scott in 1848. It was occupied by Army Dragoons who were mounted infantry and the Fort was in this location to protect settlers in the area from hostile Comanches and members of other area tribes. However, the resourceful German immigrants who settled the area soon made their own peace treaty with the local tribes and the mutual respect between the parties rendered the fort useless. It was ultimately closed in 1866. When I visited the site I took pictures and conducted an EVP session, but nothing showed up to indicate that the post is haunted. However, I may have been in the wrong location.

According to Elaine Coleman, who wrote the book "**Texas Haunted Forts**" in 2001, the most often sighted apparitions are of mounted soldiers moving toward the hill above the fort where the historic peace treaty was signed. There have also been reports by people who have seen the German settlers, the soldiers, and the Indians engaging in the discussions on the hill that led to the ultimate accord.

CHAPTER XXX

THE GHOSTS IN BANDERA, TEXAS

The people who live in Bandera have numerous ghost stories to tell. Not far from town is historic Bandera Pass that was the location of many fights between the Indian tribes that inhabited the vast Texas Hill Country and the Spanish intruders from Mexico and then the Anglo settlers who sought to claim the area as their own. At one point the Spanish even posted a red flag on top of one of the hills in the pass that established a border between Indian and Spanish territory. However, settlers continued to move into the area and the Spanish lost control. Many of these settlers died in ambushes in the pass.

The most famous battle in the pass was fought after the Texans secured their independence from Mexico. In 1840 the Comanche Indians under the leadership of Buffalo Hump made a major raid into the towns of Victoria and Linnville, Texas, killing Texans and sacking the towns. The President of the Texas Republic, Sam Houston, ordered a company of Texas Rangers under the command of Captain John Coffee Hays to move into the area to contain the Comanches. As the company of about 50 men moved into Bandera Pass they were attacked by a large war party consisting of hundreds of Comanche Indians.

The Rangers dismounted and went into battle against overwhelming odds. They held their ground and eventually killed a prominent Comanche Chief. This led to the withdrawal of the remaining Indians. Even today people who go through the pass, particularly at night, report hearing the sounds of battle, and see mysterious orbs of light on top of the hills where the Comanches were firing from. Yet, the most common reports of supernatural activity revolve around a wagon full of settlers trying to flee from an Indian ambush. Modern ranchers in the area will find the ruts of wagon wheels in their fields near the pass, as if the settlers are continuing in their quest to avoid the marauding Indians, and go on with their journey.

As you walk down the main street of Bandera itself you may see the cowboys from the area ranches riding their horses into town during the late afternoon to visit one of the saloons for a well earned drink or two. They tie their horses up to the hitching posts in front of the saloons and to the casual observer it may seem like you have just walked through a time warp into the days when major cattle drives started in Bandera and made their way to the railroads in Dodge City, Kansas or other locations. However, these are not ghosts, but modern cowboys.

One of the must visit locations on the main street in Bandera is the "General Store" where you can browse through a variety of fascinating western merchandise, indulge in a coke float or chocolate malt at the old fashioned soda fountain, and hear stories about Henry, the resident ghost. The store is owned by Bob and Gail Click. Bob is a retired U.S. Marine Corps Colonel and did not impress me as the type of individual who would believe in the supernatural unless he had experienced firsthand encounters. However, in my conversations with him I learned that such encounters are frequent in the General Store and Bob is definitely a believer. That is primarily due to the fact that Henry is one very active ghost, and is not shy about making his presence known to the owners and employees of the store as well as to customers.

Henry has been known to blow his hot breath on Bob's neck. Gail didn't believe in such things as ghosts until one day in the store when she felt a presence behind her and heard a deep gruff voice "what are you doing here?" When she turned and nobody was there she headed quickly into the office to get away from whatever it was that had spoken to her. Henry delights in being mischievous and one night after the store was closed Bob heard Christmas music playing throughout the store when nothing was turned on that could have accounted for it. He finally traced the source to a Christmas book that of course contained nothing that could account for the music. Another morning as the store was being opened, a battery operated bottle opener that had not worked in months began playing a Spanish song "Cervesa Por Favor" and again, there was no rational explanation for this.

One morning when Bob's sister and a friend of hers were in the store and talking negatively about men, a heart shaped fan flew across the store in their direction. Apparently Henry doesn't like women, or at least resents it when they have some disparaging comments to make about the male gender. Of course, it also appears that he just likes to get attention by throwing things. One day when several customers were

...ng the store's merchandise a picture of a cowgirl bathing in a tub went flying across the back of the store. There is a bell on the front door that rings when customers enter or leave the store, but it also frequently rings when the door is closed and no one is going in or out. Cowbells that are for sale on shelves in the store will also start ringing on their own. Henry likes to knock things off of the soda fountain late at night which the employees don't appreciate because they have to clean up his mess when they open up in the morning.

On one occasion when Bob was being interviewed by a female reporter about the strange happenings in the store a disembodied voice made some comments to her. The reporter had entered the store as a skeptic, but was convinced of Henry's existence when she left. The incident had definitely gotten her attention. On another occasion Bob was telling the ghost stories to a customer at the soda fountain when the bell on the door started to ring without anyone coming in or out. The customer was not impressed and said that there must be a string behind the counter that was used to ring the bell. He was invited to search for it and found nothing. His skepticism also disappeared.

Not far from the General Store there is another store called "Old West Imports" where visitors can check out a vast selection of western and Mexican merchandise brought in from many locations. I spent some time with Tillie Smith, one of the owners, and she told me some stories about a ranch that she and her husband Bob once owned outside of Bandera on St. Geronimo Creek off of Texas Hwy 16. They had purchased the land and constructed a house and almost immediately strange things started happening.

The first major incident occurred one night when the boys had gone coon hunting with their father. Tillie's niece was staying with them at the time and had her new baby with her. The niece had been sick and the following morning Tillie said her niece had asked her if she had come upstairs to her room to check on the baby. Tillie said that she had not been upstairs and the niece reported that she had seen a woman come into the room, lean over the crib and cover the baby. They had no idea who it was since they were the only people in the house at that time.

The second incident to get everyone's attention was when Tillie's nephew and his new bride came to spend some time with them. They were newly married and could not really afford a honeymoon so the Smith's let them come to their home in the country. On their first night at the home they were awakened by the sight and sound of a man and woman standing at the foot of their bed laughing at the newlyweds. They initially thought it was Tillie and her husband but were informed the next morning that the couple would certainly not have disturbed these young people on their wedding night. The identity of the laughing man and woman remains a mystery.

After this second appearance by apparitions in the home the hauntings began to progress at an accelerated pace. Tillie's granddaughter saw an elderly woman working in the kitchen who just vanished into thin air. As some ghosts made visual appearances in one form or another others just got noisy. Tillie said that she and her husband would sometimes go to bed at night in the master bedroom that was in the downstairs area of the house. After the lights were turned out they would hear the sounds of the furniture upstairs being moved around and doors slamming. The sounds were unmistakable. It was always clear that heavy pieces of furniture were being pushed around the upstairs rooms. Yet when Tillie and her husband would go upstairs everything would be in perfect order. Nothing had been moved. This continued night after night.

As unnerving as all of this was, Tillie told me that none of it really frightened her. However, that all changed one night when she got up to go to the bathroom and things got very weird. Upstairs in the home there were three windows and one of them was designed to send sunshine right into the downstairs area. However, since the home the Smith's had built was out in the woods well off of the main highway there were no lights that would shine though that window at night. That is until this night. Suddenly, Tillie found herself bathed in a bright light that came from outside and lit up the entire house. Yet, there was no light source that could have caused this. Tillie said she prayed that if this was something evil for the Lord to take it away and eventually the light faded. An explanation for the light was never found.

Tillie's daughter spent her early years on the ranch and had an imaginary friend called George. At least Tillie and her husband assumed it was an imaginary friend. However, on one occasion they had taken pictures of a motorcycle they had outside of the house and when the photographs were developed there was the apparition of a soldier in the background of one of the pictures. Perhaps this is George. When Hwy 16 between Bandera and San Antonio was being widened there were ruins of an Indian village found. This soldier might have been in one of the fights between the U.S. Army and the Indians that occurred frequently in Texas. His spirit may have moved into this new ranch house when it was built, but only Tillie's daughter could actually see him.

Across the street from the General Store in Bandera is another western gift shop called the "Branding Iron." I talked to Vicki at the store and she told me that the store is often visited by Gail and Bobby who were two old friends of hers that she had known for 25 years. Both of them have passed away but she knows they are the ones who knock things off of the wall and rearrange merchandise to let her know that they are still with her. She can often feel their presence in the store and she considers them her guardian angels. In fact, she told me that on several occasions as she was ready to leave the store her friends have made their presence felt and she knows they were telling her to delay her departure. Both times she learned later that there had been an accident on her route home at about the time she would have been in the area had she left the store when she was first planning to.

Probably the most haunted site in Bandera is the old jail that now houses the offices of the Bandera County River Authority. This is a beautiful old stone building that overlooks the Medina River and as is the case with many south Texas locations has a ghost with a name. In this case the resident spirit is named Harvey, although I personally believe that there may be more than one ghost that is involved with the numerous supernatural activities in the building. I first heard about Harvey and his activities form Stephanie who is a reporter for a local newspaper, the Bandera Courier. She and another reporter spent the night in the old jail house not long ago and had some very frightening experiences.

The first thing that Stephanie and the other reporter heard was a sound like metal striking rocks. This is not surprising since throughout the portion of the building where the cells were there are carvings in the stone walls and floor. These were done by prisoners who had plenty of idle time on their hands so they amused themselves by using whatever they could find to carve their names into the stones. I saw these carvings for myself when I visited the jail.

Sometime later that night the two women heard a loud crash on the second floor of the building where the cells were located. It sounded like a large box or something similar had hit the floor hard. They rushed to the area where the noise had come from and they could find nothing that could have created that much of a crash. In fact, they could find nothing at all that could have fallen. Finally the two intrepid reporters fell asleep and about 3:00 a.m. they both woke up at the same time and saw a dark shadow of someone or something pass in front of them.

That experience confirmed something that had initiated their investigation in the first place. They had been told that employees were coming into the offices of the River Authority in the morning to find that someone had turned on the computers overnight and been surfing the Internet. No one could figure out how someone had managed to get into the building since there was never any sign of a break in so it was decided to set up video cameras to try and catch the culprit in the act. However, the only thing the cameras ever picked up was a dark shadow crossing in front of them at precisely 3 o'clock every morning. This was exactly what the reporters had seen at exactly the same time of the morning.

Another thing that Stephanie and her friend heard that night was a loud crack like that of a gunshot. However, they weren't sure at the time and it was several months later that they learned that in fact someone had been shot dead years ago in the old Bandera Ice House which is right near the jail. Harvey continues to be active and in fact the cleaning crew that used to come at night will no longer enter the building after dark. There have been too many instances where strange noises have been heard and lights mysteriously go off and on by themselves.

After I concluded my interview with Stephanie I headed directly for the old jail where I spent some time with the very friendly General Manager of the Bandera County River Authority, David Jeffery. He told me that there have been a number of unexplained things that have happened in the old building and one of the first things he mentioned confirmed what the reporters had heard. He and others who work in the structure have heard the loud crash of what sounds like a large box being dropped on the floor. Yet when they search the premises they can't find anything that could account for the noise. He even set up an audio recorder one night that picked up the same banging noise, yet nothing could be found the next morning out of place.

David has heard the sounds of what appear to be people talking in the building when he is working alone late in the evening, and even when he has had the door to his office closed he has heard the distinct sound of footsteps like someone has just walked by his office. Yet, when he goes to investigate the building is empty and he can find no explanation of the voices or the footsteps. He also confirmed that they can't get anyone to come in and clean the building at night. The cleaning has to be done during the day because there are just too many strange things that occur after dark.

After making this visit and walking around the outside of the building both at night and during the day I have developed my own theory about who Harvey might be. The jail was built in 1881 and while there are no records of any executions of prisoners there is an old oak tree right outside of the jail that would make a perfect hanging tree. In fact, when I first walked by it and looked at the large limb that hangs over an embankment sloping down to the river I had the immediate impression that someone had died hanging from that tree. David has often wondered about the possibility of executions at that spot. There is another possible location where a live oak tree used to exist but was cut down for some reason. After all, this was a Wild West town where a lynching or two may have occurred when people were too impatient to wait for a Circuit Judge to hold a trial and pronounce sentence on someone that the locals considered guilty of a heinous crime. Harvey could be the restless and unhappy spirit of one such victim.

There are many attractions in Bandera and included among them are the many saloons that are all over this small town. The most famous is Arkey Blue's Silver Dollar because it is the oldest continuously operating Honky Tonk in the State of Texas. It is on Main Street below the General Store. Another favorite watering hole is the 11th Street Cowboy Bar that is just a block off of Main Street. Along with the other saloons in town it has live country/western music every weekend and some of the most famous Country/Western stars in the country have appeared on the large outdoor stage at the saloon.

The 11th Street Cowboy Bar is the place where bikers, cowboys, and tourists mingle and it is also a favorite spot for many veterans and active duty military personnel from the San Antonio area. The bar also has the reputation of being haunted. It was opened sometime in the 1930s and I have consumed my share of beer in the saloon on my visits to Bandera. I recently had the opportunity to talk to Dawn who is the bar manager and is also a retired 20 year veteran of the United States Air Force. She and other bartenders told me that the saloon gets downright eerie when they are closing up at night.

Footsteps will be heard when there is no one else in the building and there are also voices that seem to come from thin air. Doors will often open and close by themselves. Dawn also told me that when she sits on the stool at the far end of the bar on the right side she often feels a dramatic drop in temperature. This occurs even after the air conditioner has been shut down for the night. Many of the employees and locals that frequent the bar feel that the resident ghost is probably "Cotton" who was the original owner of the saloon. Legend has it that Cotton really enjoyed owning a bar and was known to be a heavy drinker and that was what ultimately caused his death. I suppose that if you own a saloon in the "Cowboy Capitol of the World" that is an appropriate way to go. In any case, the employees often feel that late at night they are not alone in the bar.

Old jailhouse in Bandera, Texas where a mischievous spirit named Harvey resides

The General Store in Bandera, Texas where a ghost called Henry hangs out

CHAPTER XXXI

MORE TEXAS HILL COUNTRY GHOSTS

In the small town of Medina, Texas there is a delightful place called "The Apple Store". It is on property where there are huge apple tree orchards and at the store you can choose from a myriad of apple themed gifts and items made from apples including pies, ice cream, and jelly. There is also a small but very good restaurant called the Patio Café connected with the store. When my friend Ann took me there for lunch one day we were both unaware that we were stepping into what would prove to be a treasure trove for Hill Country ghost stories.

The store was originally a residence and apparently some of the former residents, who are now deceased, continue to hang out on the premises. They are probably just checking things out to see that their former home is being treated with the proper respect. Mary, who is one of the employees of the café, told me that on one occasion she was taking a video in the cafe' and after shooting the interior of the eatery she turned to film the outside back door. She didn't see anyone until she looked at the video and there was clearly a man standing in the doorway. She said that she did not see him when she was filming and he was not one of the patrons or employees who were on the premises at the time. This gentleman has also been seen by employees at night. He appears most often as a shadowy figure moving in and out of the door to the café and also in and out of the door to the kitchen.

Mary also reports that she and some of the other employees have felt someone tap them on the shoulder when there is no one near them. She also had to dodge a fingernail file that flew off of a shelf in the building and came right at her one night. Inside the store I talked to Phila who told me that at one time the area she worked in was just a screened in porch and an elderly woman had her bedroom in this area. She is apparently still around and likes to help out in the store. Phila says that she will often come into the store in the morning and find that merchandise on the shelves has been rearranged during the night when the store is locked up tight.

While I was at "The Apple Store" I also talked to a young man named Joe who was enjoying lunch in the Patio Café. He told me that his parents own a Mexican restaurant in Mission, Texas. One of the previous residents of the premises before it became a restaurant was a woman who had lost her children when they were taken away by her husband. She apparently went insane after this incident and eventually died. Her ghost has been seen roaming around on the back patio of the establishment by Joe's parents and employees of the restaurant. They will often catch fleeting glimpses of a woman in the area when there is no one fitting that description in the restaurant. Joe says that on one occasion his father was in the back of the restaurant where the ice machine was. He was loading up bags of ice when he felt the definite presence of someone standing behind him, yet there was no one there. As he walked away he felt a blast of cold air on him, but again there was nothing there that could have caused it.

Another small town not far from San Antonio is Boerne, Texas. It was originally settled by German immigrants and is rich in its heritage. The antique shops and historic sites make it well worth a visit. A great place to stay is Ye Kendall Inn that was first established in 1859 by Erastus and Sarah Lee who rented rooms to horsemen and stage coach travelers. It became an important stop on the Stage Coach line. There were many subsequent owners throughout the years but it continued as a stage coach stop throughout the 1800s, yet one of the original owners, Sarah Lee, apparently still considers it her private domain. She continues to make her presence known even to this day.

One of the rooms in the hotel is named for her and a few years ago she was seen sitting at the hotel bar. Her presence was noticed by the bartender and all of the patrons in the bar at that time before she simply faded away. This incident was so dramatic that it was reported on one of the local television stations. Sarah harms no one, but continues to make her presence felt especially in and around the room that bears her name.

Just outside of Bandera there is a little community called Pipe Creek and near it is a small Methodist Church known as Polly's Chapel. It is a beautiful old stone church that was constructed in 1882 by Jose Policarpo (Polly) Rodriquez. Polly was a colorful figure in the history of the Texas hill country. He was born in Mexico in 1829 and in 1841 his family moved to San Antonio, Texas. During his lifetime Polly was a guide and scout for the U.S. Army, an Indian fighter, a pioneer, a rancher, and a Methodist preacher.

In 1858 Polly bought 360 acres of land along Privilege Creek and started his career as a successful rancher. It was while ranching that he converted from Catholicism to being a Methodist and the church gave him a license to serve as a Minister in 1878. His Chapel is still in service today and is open to the public to visit. It is also available for weddings. Polly died in 1914 and is buried in a small cemetery near the Chapel.

While in Bandera I talked to several people who have visited the cemetery and they relayed to me that they always felt the presence of someone else in the cemetery when they were there, although they never actually saw any of these spirits. Perhaps what they felt was the spirit of Polly, still watching over his domain. When I was there during the day I had the same feeling that I was not alone, even though no living person was present with me.

I had a similar and more dramatic experience when I visited another old Texas cemetery. This one is not in the Hill Country, but is not far from my home in Carrollton, Texas. The Baccus Cemetery is in Plano, Texas, now a thriving city that is a suburb of Dallas. Plano became part of Texas in 1840 and grew steadily until the Civil War. After the war, it struggled to survive and rebuild, but in 1870 virtually the entire town was destroyed in a fire. However, it was rebuilt again and continued to grow. The cemetery is over 200 years old and is reported to be very haunted. In the book "**Ghosts in the Graveyard; Texas Cemetery Tales**" by Olyve Hallmark Abbott there are tales related of persistent cold spots and visitors feeling the presence of someone coming up behind them, yet, when they turn around there is no one there.

When I visited the cemetery one evening I immediately noticed that it is eerily quiet, despite the fact that it is completely surrounded by a bustling outdoor mall called the "Shops at Legacy" named for Legacy Drive which runs through the mall and past the cemetery. The graveyard is small enough that when I was there I could see that no one else was present and I could hear nothing of the activity in the mall.

There are many local veterans of America's wars buried there and so as I walked through it I turned on my recorder and decided to do an EVP session. One of the first places I stopped was at the grave of a U.S. Army private who was killed in 1943 during WW II. I recited the information about this American hero into my recorder and then left it on as I continued walking. I heard nothing, but when I played back the tape later there I heard the distinct sound of someone walking beside me whistling. Yet, I was still alone in the cemetery when this occurred. The graveyard also contains the remains of a number of young children and later in the same EVP session I picked up the clear sounds of children laughing and playing. Yet, I was still alone in the cemetery when these events occurred.

Ye Kendall Inn in Boerne, Texas

CHAPTER XXXII

CASTROVILLE, TEXAS

The small and very historic town of Castroville is located approximately 25 miles west of San Antonio and like many of the small towns in and around the Texas Hill Country it has its own unique heritage. The town was founded in 1844 by a Frenchman named Henri Castro who brought over a number of colonists from the Rhenish provinces in France, especially from the Alsace-Lorraine area. Castro was to receive a land grant of over one million acres from the Republic of Texas on the condition that he settle at least 600 families on the grant within three years. The migration to the land grant started in 1842 and within two years there were over seven hundred colonists receiving land in the area and the town of Castroville was officially established near the Medina River. Within a few years many additional settlers came to the area and three more small towns were established on the original land grant.

A large number of historic buildings have been carefully preserved in Castroville and there are some fine Bed and Breakfast establishments to attract visitors to spend some time in the town and take the historic walking tour. On a Sunday in August each year the first church established in the town, St Louis Catholic Church hosts what it calls "The Granddaddy of all Church Festivals." It attracts thousands of visitors from all over the region. Of course, a town with this much history also has its share of ghosts.

During my recent visit to the area I was again escorted by my friends Bob and Ann who sometimes assist me in my research by actively looking for haunted spots all around the Hill Country in south Texas. For several years Ann has been trying to find places for me to ghost hunt in Castroville since there were no possibly haunted locations listed in any book. When she made inquiries around the town she was always told that there were no ghosts in the town. As soon as I arrived at the airport Ann told me that we needed to have lunch at a place in Castroville called the Old Alsatian Steakhouse and Ristorante because she had a surprise for me. After some excellent food, lunch quickly turned into a marathon session of ghost hunting where I was treated to many stories connected with the building. We had finally broken the "Code of Silence" surrounding the ghosts of Castroville

The restaurant is in the original structure of what was once a house consisting of a single room and a cellar. It was built around 1865 by Joseph and Catherine Krust. Joseph was later killed in an Indian raid and Catherine sold the house to Joseph Carle who added to the building and operated a General Store out of it for many years. As part of the original deal with Catherine, the Carle family also built an apartment that they rented to Catherine for $1.00 per year for the rest of her life.

It is generally believed that it is Catherine who is the primary spirit haunting the house. This is partially due to the fact that while Joseph is buried in the Castroville cemetery, Catherine is not and that indicates she was probably buried behind the house. In addition, a little girl's ghost has been seen and this was probably the young daughter of Joseph and Catherine. During excavations to add a patio to the structure, the headstone of the grave of a child was found. If her daughter died in the home and was buried on the grounds it stands to reason that Catherine is still there to take care of her.

Catherine's one room apartment with a porch and kitchen is actually the cellar of an additional wing of the house added by Joseph Carle. It is now a wine cellar and a room used for wine tasting parties. However, Catherine is still around keeping an eye on things and frequently makes her presence known to the owners of the restaurant as well as employees and guests. One of the employees has actually witnessed the apparition of a woman come though the locked doors of the cellar, go up the steps, walk across the courtyard and then pass through the closed metal gates.

A former male employee said that when he was on the same stairs he saw the apparition and she actually walked right through him. It shook him up considerably and he pointed out to the owner that he smelled like rosewater after the incident. The owner confirmed that the odor of the strong cologne he usually wore had been replaced by the clear fragrance of rosewater which is the scent that Catherine would probably have worn. This same man stated that prior to this incident he had seen the woman often on the stairs or in the storage room, but this was his only physical encounter with her.

I also heard the story of the Castroville Hearse which is in a museum in San Antonio and has been featured on the History Channel in the show America's Most Haunted. The doors of the hearse are often found open when there was no one in the building to have opened them. They are very heavy doors and cannot open on their own. The hearse was filmed on several occasions. The film would suddenly be scrambled and within 30 seconds the film would be clear again and the doors to the hearse would be opened despite the fact that there was no one near it that could have opened the doors.

I next interviewed the daughter of the owners of the restaurant, a delightful young lady named Alex Smith who took me on a tour of the restaurant and grounds and told me many stories including several about her personal encounters with the resident ghosts. She said that there are often reports from people walking by the wine cellar who hear voices when there is no one else present. She also told me that there was an employee who had worked in the restaurant before Alex's parents bought it said she once saw the apparition of a small boy standing in front of one of the mirrors. He apparently disappeared when she approached him.

It might be the little boy, the young female ghost that has been seen, or even Catherine herself who gets mischievous and plays around with the machines in the upstairs office that is over the old general store. The spirit particularly likes to run the tape in the adding machine out so that when the office is opened in the morning the adding machine paper is all over the floor. Prior to this being the office for the business it was a residence and people who lived there reported hearing footsteps when they were alone, the sound of a rocking chair in the bedroom even though there was no rocking chair on the premises, and the rather startling sound like that of a bowling ball rolling down the stairs.

Alex had her own strange encounter on the stairs. As she was about to ascend the stairs to the office she had a flash of a little girl in a long white dress tumbling head first down the stairs. This could be the way Catherine's daughter died and Alex may have seen a replay of a tragedy that occurred over 100 years ago. On another occasion Alex and several of her friends were upstairs in the office using the computer. When they got ready to leave they could not open the door that would take them to the stairs. It appeared to be locked, but the lock was on the inside where they were and they could not get it unlocked. At the same time there was a dramatic drop in the temperature in the room and it turned freezing cold. Alex finally had to call her mother who came up and used her key to unlock the door from the outside and let the young people out of the room.

Alex next told me about the old saloon that is now the house where she and her family live. It was an active saloon for many years and according to the locals on one occasion a gunfight occurred right in front of the saloon. It involved several drunken patrons of the saloon and two local Sheriff Deputies. Both of the deputies were killed and it is said that on nights when there is a full moon people have seen the two deputies walking in front of the saloon as if they are still conducting their nightly patrols. Alex has never witnessed this first hand but she did tell me that she feels very safe in that house.

However, that is not the case with the family's previous residence in the Hondo, Texas area. It is actually located in Quihi, another small Texas town founded by Castro. The house was once a stage coach stop where several fights occurred involving the owners of the stage coach stop and marauding Indians. In the cellar of the house there are gun portals cut into the walls where the defenders fired their rifles and pistols at the raiders. Inside the house there are two bullet holes in the wall next to the stairs leading to the second floor. This was the result of a gunfight that involved the local Sheriff and an outlaw he shot in the building.

Alex said she never felt comfortable in that house. She often had nightmares and other times would feel like someone was watching her. When her parents bought the restaurant in Castroville they often left Alex alone in the house until late at night when they would finally return home from working on renovations to the restaurant. Alex said that on one occasion she was watching television when she felt a presence behind her and she felt that it was that of an elderly woman who had died in the house many years before. She has also felt the presence of a Sheriff's deputy who died in the building at one time. However, her most frightening experience came one night when she experienced the presence of an Indian in the house. This scared her to the point where she actually had to leave the house. Alex impressed me as someone who is very vulnerable to psychic experiences. I do not believe she has just imagined this, she has had real experiences and she says her father is also someone who has had similar experiences.

The Smith family still owns the house, but they have since moved to Castroville and seldom stay at their old residence. However, they have a house keeper who comes in several times a month to keep up the home. She has reported constantly feeling like there is another presence in the house watching her. This confirms what Alex has experienced. Alex also said that at one point her parents were considering putting a tin roof on the house because of the number of shingles that were being blown off by the wind. However, a friend of Alex's mother is a psychic who knew nothing about the history of the house, but when visiting it told the family that Miss Emily objected to the house having a tin roof. Emily was the name of the woman who died in the house. The friend of the family was not even aware that a tin roof was being considered. The tin roof was never installed.

Alex also told me about some strange occurrences in the Lady's bathroom in the restaurant in Castroville. At one point the family had purchased an ornate mirror to hang in the bathroom. They installed it and the next day they found it turned around in the bathroom and shattered. It would have taken considerable strength to do this yet there was no way someone could have gained access to the building to make this happen; at least not anyone who was human. Alex had a kitten that refused to enter the bathroom. If the cat was placed inside of it she would go crazy, scratching and clawing the door to get back out.

My next interview in the restaurant was with Lynette Hester who works in the upstairs office. She says that she often hears footsteps when she is alone in the office. She also said that she hears the sounds of the doors opening and closing when they are not moving. In fact, earlier on the very day I interviewed her, June 25, 2010 she had her young children with her and they were in the bedroom of the former residence watching TV. One of the children came out and said "Mommy, that is a really neat bed, it moves by itself." A few weeks before her daughter had said that she constantly heard footsteps in the room when no one was present. She refuses to come up to the office any more. Lynette also confirmed Alex's reports about mischievous activities in the office including the tapes from the adding machine and also the computer getting weird on occasion.

Lynette informed me that in the bathroom next to the office where she works she keeps lipstick and other personal items. Someone or something is always moving her lipstick around. It often disappears and then reappears. This mischievous spirit is enjoying playing tricks. Lynette said that one night there a group having a wine tasting party in the wine cellar of the Alsatian Restaurant when they saw the figure of a woman come up from the wine cellar and walk through a closed door. They were so shaken by the experience that they left and have never come back. Lynette pointed out to me that even in Catherine's bedroom there are gun portals so she could shoot at any Indian raiders who appeared. Lynette says that it is standard procedure for her to say good morning to Catherine when she enters the office in the morning. Catherine is always felt to be present.

All of this occurred in Castroville near what appears to have been the site of a U.S. Army outpost. Ann told me that this was the site of a fort and there seems to be a parade ground and the buildings of an army outpost. One of the locals disputes this and said that it was only the site of a hospital and while there was a hospital there a recent excavation by a team of archeologists from Texas A&M University has uncovered a number of artifacts on the grounds of the restaurant. These include bridals labeled US, pistol holsters from the Army, and a belt buckle that I believe indicates that a company of dragoons was once stationed here. This is in line with the fact that Dragoons were employed in this area prior to the Civil War to defend settlers against Comanche Indian attacks. Lynette took me to the excavation site and to the old smokehouse next to it. The smokehouse is really a concrete blockhouse that also served as a fortress for the family during Indian raids. There are numerous gun portals in the brick walls. The smokehouse was specifically built so that it can't be burned down.

Lynette had a wealth of information for me and mentioned that her in-laws are direct descendants of the founders of Castroville and they have a home in the area where there have been a number of paranormal incidents. A man died in that house and she and other members of the family have been present in the house when glasses would actually fly off of the table, an indication that he is still present in the house.

CHAPTER XXXIII

BERCLAIR MANSION

The Berclair Mansion is actually a 22 room, two story home in the small town of Berclair, Texas that is between San Antonio and Corpus Christi. It was built in 1936 by a wealthy widow, Etta Wilkinson Terrell, who was part of large family that had been raised in the area. The original home had burned down in 1898 and Etta was determined to build a luxury home for her and her siblings that would be fireproof. She also filled the home with antiques and artwork she acquired from Europe through dealers in New Orleans

She was 75 years old when the house was built and she lived there with her four sisters and the two children of one of the sisters, also a widow, until Etta died in 1957 at the age of 95. The last of the sisters passed away in 1968. The house was abandoned for over 20 years with all of the beautiful and expensive furnishings intact and untouched. The Beeville Art Association ultimately acquired the house and it provides tours as well as the opportunity for people to rent the home for weddings and other functions.

The house is well known for its ghosts and was investigated by professional paranormal investigators on one occasion. This was Miss Etta's home and she continues to watch over it. On one recent tour a woman informed the staff that she was a psychic and that Etta had given her a message for the members of the Art Society. She wanted them to know that she did not like the new color they had painted her bedroom and there was a piece of furniture removed that she wanted back. Unfortunately, she didn't specific what was removed that she wants returned.

All of the sisters had their bedrooms upstairs and that was considered the lady's part of the house. It was off limits to men who might be visiting the home including the son of one of the sisters. He had his own bedroom downstairs. This is apparently a rule that Etta continues to try to enforce. When the ghost hunting team, which consisted entirely of men, was upstairs conducting an EVP session they heard a woman's voice clearly order them to "get out." This statement can be heard on the recording they made. However, the researchers did pick up the sounds of men's voices in the house and made contact with the ghost of a young man who apparently inhabits the attic of the home.

He identified himself only as Adams and was apparently a deserter from the army. He stated that this was in 1836 and since that is the time of the Texas revolution against Mexico it can be assumed that he was AWOL from the army of Texas. He also said his mother lived in this area. He claimed to have been at a party before he died. However, there seems to be no direct connection with the time period after the house was built so he may have been on the property at a much earlier time and just decided that the attic of this new home was a nice place to occupy.

After the tour I got permission from the lovely ladies of the Beeville Art Association to do my own EVP session in the attic. I tried to make direct contact with Adams and while I got no verbal responses I did get a strange whistling sound in response to some of my questions. This could only be heard on the tape and I didn't hear it at all when I was in the attic. There were certainly no birds in there with me and there was no sound of wind blowing through the room. The attic is not very large so I stood right in the middle of it and did not move. However, at one point the tape picked up the unmistakable sound of footsteps approaching me and stopping right next to me. This proceeded the whistling. Another thing that occurred was that when I opened the door to the attic the light came on before I could touch the switch. It appeared that I was expected and I was being welcomed into the room.

There is also some evidence that young Adams may have found other parts of the house to his liking. When the mansion was acquired by the Art Association there was considerable work that had to be done before the home could be opened to the public. When the mansion was built Etta made sure that all of the latest amenities were added to the house. She had electricity installed and in fact in a very generous gesture to the town she paid for the power company to provide electrical service to the entire surrounding community of Berclair. She also had an elevator installed in her home to make life easier for her and her siblings.

When the house was being prepared to reopen, electricians were called in to make sure everything worked properly. On one occasion one of the men told his partner that when going upstairs they needed to be quiet because there was a man sleeping in one of the bedrooms. He was informed that this was impossible since the only other person in the house was the woman from the Art Association who had unlocked the door for the electricians. However, the man insisted that he had seen a man asleep on one of the beds and about a year later when he was called out to work on the elevator again he repeated the story and said that he had made no mistake. Perhaps one of the beds in one of the bedrooms formally occupied by the sisters is particularly appealing to the resident army deserter.

In addition to the work being done inside of the house before it was opened to the public there was a great deal to be done outside. This included landscaping and the laying of brick walkways. The workers doing this arrived very early in the morning and a few hours later members of the Art Association would come to the mansion to provide lemonade to the workers and make sure they got lunch. About two weeks into the project one of the workers mentioned to a lady providing lunch to him that he wanted to thank the woman who lived in the house for always being so friendly to them when they arrived in the morning. He was informed that no one lived in the house, but he insisted that every morning when he arrived there was a woman in the window of one of the upstairs bedrooms who waved at him and he always waved back. The window they are talking about is the bedroom window of one of the sisters.

I found this particularly interesting because when my friends and I had arrived at the mansion and were walking up to the door Ann and I both saw a woman in one of the windows waving at us. We were told that no one was upstairs at that time. After we had been at the mansion for several hours I examined the window where we had seen someone and found that it was closed with a double set of curtains. I later found out that my friend Bob had done the same thing during the tour. Therefore we could not have seen a reflection from a mirror or anything else in the room. When we walked outside and were preparing to leave we could still see the form of someone or something in the window. We took pictures from several angles and tried to determine if this was a reflection off of the glass. However, the angle of the sun at that time could not have caused a reflection off of the glass of the window, yet it was still there and showed up in the pictures we took with a digital camera. This is something that clearly remains unexplained.

While on the tour we were also shown a remarkable photograph that was taken in the upstairs hallway. Several women of the Art Association were photographed when they were putting old books into a glass enclosed book case. The photo clearly shows the women and also has the reflection in the glass of the person taking the picture. There is also the reflection of a fourth person standing behind the photographer. Yet, there was no fourth person in the hallway at the time.

Another interesting phenomenon occurred when we left of Etta's bedroom. As Bob walked into the room he felt a blast of cold air blast through him as if someone was passing through him to follow the tour. Of course, since he was a man in the forbidden upstairs portion of the house, there is also the possibility that he was being encouraged to leave this part of the ladies' home as soon as possible. In any case, when we had finished spending almost five hours in this beautiful home, we were all convinced that there were several spirits still there that have no intention of leaving.

Female ghost seen in upstairs window of the Berclair Mansion

CHAPTER XXXIV

HAUNTED CORPUS CHRISTI

The next stop on the tour of haunted places in south Texas was the coastal city of Corpus Christi. The first night there we went to Blackbeard's Restaurant. This restaurant has been around on the Corpus Christi Beach for years. It was originally just a bar and the legend is that in 1955 there was a fight in the bar over an attractive redhead from New Orleans. When the fight ended one of the men involved lay dead and it is suspected that it is his ghost that haunts the site.

However, during the depression in the 1930s there was a work camp in the area and one of the men working from it came to the bar every night. He had recently lost his beloved wife and was clearly despondent over her death. One night he left the bar and went back to the camp where he committed suicide. He could also still be present in the bar and restaurant.

Over the years the staff members at the restaurant have reported hearing voices in the restaurant when all the customers have gone, as well as instances of lights going off and on, chairs moving by themselves, and items like salt and pepper shakers flying around the room on their own. Someone also takes great delight in playing with the thermostat and setting it from freezing cold to blazing hot. I was at the restaurant on June 26, 2010 and had some very good seafood.

I then talked to David Perez, a night manager of the restaurant who told me about an incident that occurred several years ago. He and the rest of the staff were preparing to close down for the night when one of the other employees told him that there was something wrong with the back door. It kept being repeatedly unlocked. David led me down the short hallway from the room where the alarm box is located to the back door. It took about 4-5 seconds to make the short walk.

When the code is punched in to set the alarm the box will indicate if a door to the restaurant is unlocked. David said that he locked the back door and then went to set the code but it informed him that the door was again unlocked. David confirmed that this was the case and locked it again. He walked back to the alarm box and found that the door had been unlocked again during this brief walk. This continued to happen and David initially thought one of the other employees was playing games with him and yelled at everyone to stay away from the door. He then realized that there was no way anyone could get to the door, unlock it, and get away from it without him seeing them.

After several frustrating minutes David finally realized that it had to be the resident spirit being mischievous so David told the ghost that he was tired and wanted to go home so would he stop playing this game. This time the door remained locked and the alarm was set.

Corpus Christi is also the home of the U.S.S. Lexington a World War II era aircraft carrier. It is open daily to visitors and you can easily spend the whole day touring it. The massive warship was built and commissioned in 1943 and was named the Lexington after the original carrier with that name was sunk by the Japanese at the Battle of the Coral Sea. The infamous Tokyo Rose reported on at least four separate occasions that the new Lexington had also been sunk by the Japanese. It was hit by a torpedo shortly after it was sent to sea for the first time and it took a devastating hit by a kamikaze in 1945, but the Japanese never came close to sinking the mighty warship. However, because of the blue color the ship was painted and the repeated stories of her demise, the ship became known as the "Great Blue Ghost".

There are walking tours you can take to see various parts of the ship and each one of them will take you through areas that are reported to be haunted. There have been many sightings over the years since the Lexington made its permanent home in Corpus Christi. Ghosts have been seen throughout the ship. In fact, I was visiting the ship on a Monday, June 28, 2010 and several employees told me about the most recent sighting that had taken place just a few days earlier on Thursday June 24th.

It involved an F-18 jet fighter plane that is part of the aircraft exhibit on the flight deck. A father and son reported seeing a pilot sitting in the cockpit of the aircraft in full flight gear. He actually waved to them and then disappeared. What makes this report particularly interesting is the fact that the jet aircraft was never on the Lexington when it was an active duty ship. The plane was part of the Navy's famous Blue Angels precision flying group that performs in air shows all over the country. Of course, like I was told, no one really knows the history of the plane. Pilots with the Blue Angels are occasionally killed in accidents during training or shows and perhaps this apparition was one of those pilots who once flew this particular plane, and followed it when it was moved to the carrier to be part of the exhibit.

There is another possibility and it is the theory I believe in. The Lexington served the U.S. Navy from 1943 until 1991. After World War II it was jet aircraft that flew from its decks and were in combat sorties over Korea and during the Vietnam War. The ghost in the F-18 could be one of those young men who was killed while serving on the carrier and may have just been checking out this newer and more advanced fighter. Whoever he is, his appearance was certainly still a hot topic of conversation when I visited the ship.

If you have never been on one of these huge aircraft carriers it is hard to imagine what they are like. When at sea the Lexington had a crew of 5,000 sailors and airmen and everyone was involved in the actions of the ship. The ship is in effect a small floating city and everyone has a specific job to do and in some cases more than one job depending on the circumstances. Sailors might be doing anything from working in the galleys where food was prepared and served to the crew, or they might be manning the anti aircraft guns that were deployed to fight off attacks by enemy aircraft.

On the other hand, the ship had its own hospital and dental clinic, it s own chapels and Post office, and the often cramped living quarters for the sailors. There are numerous decks on the ship and moving from one location to another involved going through narrow passageways, up or down flights of steep steps, and through numerous hatches that were often sealed when the battle stations were manned and the ship was engaged in combat operations.

During World War II the Lexington carried and launched three types of aircraft against the Japanese. There were torpedo planes for use against enemy ships, bombers to attack enemy vessels or to support Marines landing on Japanese held islands, and sleek fighter planes to protect the torpedo planes and bombers or provide close air support for troops on the ground. There were squadrons on board the ship that contained a compliment of each type of aircraft. Many brave men lost their lives while flying operations off of the Lexington during WW II and some of them seem to still be on board. When they were waiting to launch the pilots and crew members of the planes often spent time in the "ready rooms" where they were briefed on upcoming operations or debriefed after they had returned from a combat operation.

The first tour I took after boarding the Lexington was Tour Number 3. I specifically chose this one because I had heard that there have been reports of ghost sightings in and around the ready rooms that are part of this tour. It also included sites like the Captain's Quarters and the all important Combat Information Center which was really the heart of the ship when it was in a combat situation. My friends Ann and Bob accompanied me on the tour and we had several strange experiences. Both of them are sensitive to the spirit world so we make a good trio on ghost hunting trips.

One of the air groups on board the Lexington during WW II was Squadron 19 and as we walked down the passageway toward the Ready Room for Bombing 19 I stepped through a hatch and immediately felt a noticeable drop in temperature and a gust of cold air pass right through me. I didn't say anything but waited for a moment as Ann passed thought the hatch and I could see by the expression on her face that she had also experienced something. When we compared notes, we found that we had both experienced the same feeling of an unseen presence in the passageway.

We entered several ready rooms during the tour but I obtained a bizarre photo at a ready room exhibit that has been set up to look just like it did during WW II. Aviators gear is draped over each chair and the maps and charts are all authentic. There is even a mannequin dressed in the uniform of a WW II pilot standing in the front of the room. The whole area is enclosed in glass so that the exhibit can't be disturbed. I had both a 35 mm camera and a digital camera and I took several pictures with each one. One of the photos on Ann's digital camera is really strange. It shows a transparent blue light engulfing one of the chairs in the ready room. There was no blue light in the room that could account for this phenomenon and a reflection for the flash of the camera would have been white, not blue. There is also what appears to be a face in the light. I have no explanation for this and neither does anyone else that has looked at the picture.

While on the Lexington I talked with the Director, Charles "Rusty" Reustle who confirmed that there is a lot of ghostly activity in the engine room, on the mess deck, and in the area where his office is located. However, the report of the apparition that is most often seen in all of these areas has one striking similarity in all of them. People who have seen this sailor often comment on his piercing blue eyes.

Rusty also mentioned that they recently had a Navy Inspector on board the ship who made it quite clear that he did not believe in ghosts. However, he had an experience during his visit that apparently changed his mind because he refused to come back on the ship to complete his inspection. According to one of the other Lexington employees the Inspector had been on the Hanger Deck in the area of the elevator that takes the planes from the Hanger Deck to the Flight Deck to be launched. During WW II a plane had been landing and was unable to stop before it reached the elevator that was still on the lower deck. The plane fell to the lower deck and the pilot was killed. When the inspector was going through each compartment in the area where this had occurred he would make his inspection, turn off the light, and then close the area off as he went to the next compartment. When he reached the end and turned around everything was wide open and all of the lights were back on. What else he may have seen was never reported, but it was enough for this once non-believer to cause him to leave the ship.

One of the experiences Rusty had in his office involved his ink pens. He has a half dozen of the same type of pens and they are the only ones that he uses. For a period of approximately five weeks when he took the cap off one of the pens and placed in on his desk while he was writing the cap would disappear. Finally when all of the caps had disappeared he cleaned out the entire office looking for the caps but could not find them. His office is the most secure on the Lexington. There are only two keys to it and when Rusty came into the office the next morning all of the pen caps were symmetrically laid out in front of the keyboard of his computer.

After talking to Rusty my next tour was on the flight deck of the Lexington. There are a number of aircraft on the deck that represent some of the planes that flew from the carrier. I immediately proceeded to the F-18 where the ghostly figure of the pilot had been so recently seen. I didn't see anyone in the cockpit but I took some pictures of the plane. On either side of the bridge there is a dual 5" gun mount inside of an enclosed turret. These are the largest and most powerful of the antiaircraft guns on the mighty warship and I went inside of the one that is open to the public. The second one is roped off and is apparently under repair so I could not enter it. However, as I walked by it I heard a knocking sound from inside the turret. Although, I could not enter it, I could see through the open hatches that no one was inside of it and so I have no way of accounting for the strange knocking sounds.

I then climbed to the bridge of the Lexington where I met one of the volunteer tour guides. He was one of the pilots who flew off the Lexington during World War II. On the outside of the aft part of the bridge there is a Japanese flag painted on the bulkhead indicating the location where the Kamikaze crashed into the carrier in 1945. A number of men were killed when this occurred and both employees and visitors to the ship often feel an intense sadness in that part of the bridge.

When I finished my tour of the flight deck I met Bob and Ann at the snack bar on the Hanger Deck so we could have some lunch. I had an opportunity to talk to one of the workers at the snack bar and she told me about two young boys who had been on the Lexington in the area near the snack bar when the ghost of a sailor appeared in front of them and then quickly disappeared. The boys were so scared by this that they left the ship and came back shortly thereafter with their parents. The young men had calmed down enough to describe the person they had seen in some detail and their description matched that of a sailor who has been seen in that area of the ship and is believed to have been killed there.

After lunch I took Tour Number 4 that led me through the engine room, the Post Office, the Sick Bay, the Damage Control Center and the Chapel. I heard some banging on the wall when I was in the area of the Post Office, but could not determine a source. When I finished the tour I had a chance to talk to a young man who does maintenance work on the Lexington. His name is Stephen and he had several stories to tell me. Groups such as Boy Scouts and Girl Scouts can arrange to spend the night on the aircraft carrier. They sleep in the crew quarters and can tour the ship.

Stephen was in the area where the groups stay putting food into a walk in freezer in preparation for the arrival of one such group when he saw a man in white pants and a white shirt walking down a passageway towards one of the bathrooms (called heads in the Navy.) He thought it was a tourist who had wandered into an area that was off limits and he followed the man to tell him he had to leave. The man turned into the head and at the same time Stephen saw one of his co-workers emerge from the restroom. He was wearing a blue shirt and shorts so could not have been the same person who had just entered. Stephen asked his buddy if he had seen the man entering the room and was informed that no one had entered. He searched the entire area and found no one there. Stephen then realized that he had seen someone in a sailor's uniform roaming the passageway that had simply disappeared before his eyes.

On another occasion the young maintenance man had been cleaning up the mess area after a tour group had eaten dinner. He and his co-worker had placed all of the chairs upside down on the tables and then left the room. As they walked down the passageway they heard a loud crashing noise in the mess area. They immediately returned only to find that the almost one hundred chairs were now off of the tables and on the floor. This had happened in only ten to fifteen seconds. Stephen also told me that he had been working in the area of the bridge where the Kamikaze plane hit and he had a very eerie feeling there.

USS Lexington docked at Corpus Christi, Texas

Jet aircraft on the deck of the USS Lexington where the ghost of a pilot
was seen in the cockpit

CHAPTER XXXV

GOLIAD, TEXAS

Fort St. Louis near the site of what is now Goliad, Texas was originally established by the French in 1685. The Karankawa Indian tribe attacked and destroyed the Fort a few years later. In 1721 the Presidio La Bahia was established by the Spanish on the site of the original Fort St. Louis and then moved and rebuilt several times before it became a permanent site in 1749 where it stills stands today. In 1836 the Texas revolution was occurring and Colonel James Fannin and his men captured the Presidio from the Mexican government and renamed it Fort Defiance. Shortly thereafter Fannin was ordered to take his command and reinforce the besieged Alamo in San Antonio. As his force left the Fort they were engaged in a battle with superior Mexican forces and were forced to surrender. General Santa Anna, the commander of the Mexican army ordered that the entire force of Texans be executed.

Only a hand full of men managed to escape the massacre and 342 Texas soldiers died. Their bodies were either burned or left to rot in the nearby woods where they were shot down. Finally, when Santa Anna had been defeated and the old fort reoccupied by Texas troops the remains were all gathered up and buried in a mass grave. Eventually a monument was erected over the grave.

With this type of history of violence it is not surprising that a lot of spirit activity is reported by both employees and visitors in the old Presidio. The fort has been fully restored and guests can actually spend the night if they want to. Those that choose to do so often see the ghost of a monk roaming around in the compound. They also hear the sounds of horses inside the Fort even though there have been none inside the walls for many years. The sounds of men screaming can be heard occasionally near the areas where the Texas troops were killed and several figures of women can be seen in the fort and near some gravesites. They are perhaps the wives or mothers of the slaughtered Texans

I was at the Presidio on June 29th during the day and took a number of pictures and did several EVP sessions. It was during one of these sessions that I got a remarkable response. I was in the mission chapel where some of the Texans were held prisoner until they were executed. I had assumed that Colonel James Fannin had been taken out in the woods with them, but I was incorrect. However, I did not find that out until after the EVP session. I learned that Colonel Fannin had been kept behind and executed right outside of the door of the chapel.

Prior to his execution he made three requests of his Mexican captors. First, he requested that he not be shot in the face and second that his belongings be sent to his family. His last request was that he be given a Christian burial. In response to these reasonable requests the Mexicans killed the Colonel by shooting him in the face, they divided up his belongings among them, and they threw Fannin's body onto the pile of other dead Texans that was then set on fire. It would be quite plausible that after such trauma the ghost of Colonel Fannin might still be in the area.

I found out that he is still present when I was in the chapel. I had taken pictures and run my recorder in the ornate little chapel and was preparing to leave. However, as I got to the door I felt a cold chill run up and down my spine and the hair on my arms and the back of my neck stood up. I knew someone was making contact with me and while it could have been anyone I specifically asked "If that was you Colonel Fannin...?" When I played the tape back a few minutes later I could clearly hear a whispered verbal response that occurs after I said those words and before I even completed my sentence. The response was "I'm here." It should be noted that the chapel was very warm, yet when I felt the Colonel make contact with me and provided the oral response to my question, I had also noticed that the temperature in the area where I was standing had dropped considerably in a matter of seconds. In other words, I was in a classic cold spot signifying the presence of a spirit.

I have played this tape for many different people and they all clearly hear the same words and they are convinced, as I am that the words were spoken by the ghost of Colonel James Fannin. It has been suggested that this occurred because at the time I was wearing my cap that said I was I U.S. Army Veteran. I received the response because I was a fellow American soldier.

CHAPTER XXXVI

TO BELIEVE OR NOT TO BELIEVE

It was about 3:00 in the morning and I was putting in an all nighter. It was time for the final exams of the 1970 spring semester at Louisiana State University and I was preparing for an Economics exam. That was tough enough but earlier in the day I had been to the funeral of one of my fraternity brothers. He had been killed three days earlier when his car had been hit by a drunk driver who ran a red light. Leroy had been on his way to the wedding reception for his sister who had just been married in a small Louisiana town.

I had known Leroy for three years, we had been Delta Tau Delta fraternity pledges together and his room in the fraternity house was one of the three on the ground floor and was right next to mine. The hallway was dimly lit and I had left my room to go to the kitchen for a cup of the strong Louisiana coffee that we always kept hot in a large urn during exam time. The small hallway was L shaped with one closed door leading to the dining room and kitchen and another closed door leading to the entrance foyer and stairs.

I wasn't paying much attention as I headed down the hall until I bumped into someone emerging from Leroy's room. I stepped back and looked up and up and realized I had literally run into my deceased friend. One second he was there and the next he had vanished. I checked both his room and the other room and they were empty, the other residents having already finished their exams and headed home for the summer. I tried to tell myself that I was just tired and had imagined the whole thing but I knew better; I had stepped into the realm of the supernatural. I was suddenly a believer and thus a ghost hunter was born.

Over the years since my encounter Leroy has been seen a number of times in the Delta Tau Delta House. I believe he is one of the spirits who haunts a specific location because he was either snatched away from a place he loved or he left unfinished business there. I think that many of these ghosts may not even be aware that they are dead. They are therefore not ready to pass on and probably exist in a form of limbo, not really sure what has happened to them. This is my theory and is certainly not based on any scientific evidence but it would explain most of the hauntings my wife and I have encountered during our ghost hunting adventures.

There was also the case of Dr. Nutt and Longview Plantation in Natchez, Mississippi. The doctor died leaving a magnificent plantation home half finished and he has haunted it ever since. Kay and I were taking the tour of the plantation several years ago when the young tour guide, who was new at the job, pointed out the old fashioned gout chair in one of the rooms. The guide mentioned that there had been some speculation that Dr. Nutt had invented the chair. My wife, who was a nurse, said that she had read that it was true, Dr. Nutt was the inventor. The young lady became quite indignant and disagreed, saying that no one knew for sure.

At that moment the lights went out and quickly back on again. We learned later from the plantation custodian that turning the lights off and on was Dr. Nutt's standard method of correcting the tour guides when they made an error in their narratives. Most of them were used to this and would just apologize to the upset spirit saying "Sorry Dr. Nutt", but our guide was too young to know that.

The ghost of Dr. Nutt is quite active around the plantation being seen most often near the cemetery or in other areas of the grounds. The plantation owners have a difficult time keeping groundskeepers because the good doctor will often appear and begin issuing orders to the workers who usually make a quick exit from the property.

There are several haunted plantations and if you visit during the spring pilgrimage when the houses are all open for tours you will hear quite a few ghost stories. The people in Natchez definitely believe in ghosts.

Bibliography

"Guide to the Haunted Pubs of Savannah" by Greg Proffit

"Scout's Guide to the Ghosts of Savannah" by Greg Proffit, 2008

"New Orleans Ghosts" by Victor C. Klein, 1993, Professional Press

"Spooky Stories From the Lone Star State" by Carol Riley Cain, 2008, Publish America, LLLP

"Ghosts, Spooks, and Sprits of South Texas" by Carol Riley Cain, 2006, Publish America, LLLP

"Ghosts of San Antonio" by Scott A. Johnson, 2009, Schiffer Publishing, LTD

"Ghosts in the Graveyard: Texas Cemetery Tales" by Olyve Hallmark Abbott, 2002, Republic of Texas Press

"Texas Haunted Forts" by Elaine Coleman, 2001, Republic of Texas Press

"Ghosts Along the Texas Coast" by Dorcia Schultz, 1995, Republic of Texas Press

"Ghost Stories of Texas" by Jo-Anne Christensen, 2001, Lone Pine Publishing

"Savannah Spectres and Other Strange Tales" by Margaret Wyatt DeBolt, 1984, The Donning Company, Publishers, Distributed by Schiffer Books, Ltd.

"Field Guide to America's Most Haunted, Book VI" by Jim Graczyk, 2007, Ghost Research Society Press

"Haunted Louisiana" by Christ L. Viviano, 1992, Tree House Press

"Georgia Ghosts: They are Among Us" by Ian Alan, 2005, Sweetwater Press

"Calico: Ghost Town" 1959, Knotts Berry Farm

Other books by Michael Connelly:

Riders in the Sky: The Ghosts and Legends of Philmont Scout Ranch, Merrill Press, 2001

The Mortarmen, Trafford Publishing, 2005

Amayehli: A Story of America, Trafford Publishing 2009

For more information about these books you can contact Michael Connelly at mrobertc@hotmail.com

ABOUT THE AUTHOR

 Michael Connelly is a retired attorney and a U.S. Army Veteran. He received his Juris Doctorate degree from Louisiana State University in 1973 and practiced law in Baton Rouge, Louisiana for 26 years and currently lives in Carrollton, Texas. He currently teaches law courses on the Internet. He is also a freelance writer and the author of three other books, "The Mortarmen" a book about his father's unit during WW II, "Riders in the Sky: The Ghosts and Legends of Philmont Scout Ranch", and a novel, "Amayehli: A Story of America".

He has been an avid part time ghost hunter and paranormal investigator for over 30 years and has encountered phenomenon all over the United States. He continues to investigate and plans on writing more about his new adventures.

CPSIA information can be obtained
at www.ICGtesting.com
Printed in the USA
FFOW02n0152150518
46657576-48748FF